On the New Tower: Dawn.

The Oleander Press
16 Orchard Street
Cambridge
CB1 1JT

www.oleanderpress.com

First published: October 1937
Second edition (revised): November 1937
Reprinted: 1952
This edition published by the Oleander Press: October 2007

ISBN: 9781909349551

Designed and typeset by Hamish Symington • www.hamishsymington.com

The publishers assume no responsibility for damage or injury resulting from the use
of this book, and do not condone or in any way encourage the practices depicted herein.

THE
NIGHT CLIMBERS
OF CAMBRIDGE

WHIPPLESNAITH

OLEANDER PRESS

Publisher's Acknowledgments

IN REPUBLISHING this book it was our original intention to produce a virtual facsimile of the second edition. Whilst this is largely so with the text, having found that we had the majority of the original negatives, it seemed a felicitous opportunity to use today's technology to show them to their best advantage. This we have done where possible and I hope you agree that, whilst keeping their authenticity, we have managed to improve clarity, impact and, especially, atmosphere. Six of the original (luckily unpopulated) images withstood all attempts to make even barely discernible reproductions and for these modern counterparts from our own Inefficient Photographer have been substituted. Although they are not marked, you will likely spot them.

It goes without saying that it requires commitment and assistance from many to bring to fruition a project like *Night Climbers* and to everyone involved I offer sincere thanks. The following Whipplesnaith devotees have, with good reason, been singled out for special gratitude: Andy Buckley who, with his accomplices, kept the book a virtual reality for the faithful at insectnation.org and provided essential contacts; Tom Whipple, who was instrumental in bringing publisher and book together and whose name alone should be ample qualification for inclusion in this list; Hamish Symington, great-nephew of the author, who marshalled into excellent order the text, designed the cover and painstakingly restored the pictures; and finally, of course, Ian Symington, Whipplesnaith's son, without whom you there would be no book in your hands at all. Thanks to all these, once again, it will be a fine night.

Foreword

I AM DELIGHTED that the Oleander Press is to bring out a new edition of *The Night Climbers of Cambridge*. Over the last twenty years I have searched many bookshops for a copy, but although everyone knows of the book I have never been able to find one. My first edition, which was given to me by my son Andrew, was irreparably damaged in a flood in 1999. I was subsequently fortunate that Colin Button of Little Stour Books in Kent was able to locate another copy for me in Canada. Hopefully, thanks to the Oleander Press, many others will now be able to enjoy the book in its new format, with the original photography enhanced by modern technology.

Whipplesnaith was the pen-name adopted by my father, Noel H. Symington, when he wrote *The Night Climbers of Cambridge* in the 1930s. He is clearly identifiable in many of the photographs, notably those on the Chapel. He is also identifiable as the Butterfly Collector who injured his hands climbing down the rope. His left hand never fully recovered, and was always numb in cold weather.

He was always very reticent about his exploits, and never revealed the names of any of the other Night Climbers, although Wilfrid Noyce, who was part of the 1953 Everest expedition, was a contemporary. My impression was that they never climbed together. Sadly, I never pressed him on the subject.

Rheumatic fever while at school at Rugby left him with a weak heart, and he never went on to achieve great mountaineering fame, although he climbed Mount Kenya on a number of occasions, including an ascent with the first lady and the first black man ever to reach the summit.

He died in May 1970 at the age of 56.

Ian Symington, 2007

"All men may dare what has by man been done."

Young

Multum in parvo

THIS BOOK could never have been written without the enthusiastic collaboration of many men, and it would be futile to try to thank them. A child cannot express gratitude to its parents for its birth, and the book cannot do more than mention the names of those who effected its creation. To save ourselves the impossible task of thanking them in any sort of order, we have drawn the names out of a hat; we will only say that every man who is included has been of inestimable service, from the climbers to the man at whose bidding we cut whole chapters without a murmur. The book thanks: Colonel M. G. (for hospitality), Colin, Frank, John H., David, George F., Mac., Eric, Pat, Jimmy, Gorgeous, Philip, Donald, Ronnie, Roy, Ducky, Martin, O'Hara, Noel, Alec, Kerry, Nares, Jim K., Willy, Stephan, Roger, John W., Douglas, John F.

Besides the above, twenty-four of whom were actually climbing or photographing with us, there have of course been many others whose kindness and sympathy have helped us. There are the half-dozen houses where beds were offered to us, and whose doors are always open. There are the friendly dons, porters and policemen and the strangers empanelled on the spur of the moment on the rare occasions when we were short of helpers. The book thanks them all; and there is no more to say.

The authors, 1937

Contents

CHAPTER ONE

Chiefly Padding

"Toute la nuit je l'entends rôder dans la gouttière"
Notre Dame de Paris

LTHOUGH IT is impossible to write a history of night climbing –
because there is no such history – the game of roof-climbing
remains the same, changing scarcely, if at all, from generation to generation. History records change, big events sandwiched
between long periods of monotony, while roof-climbing – if it could
stand out of the darkness which enshrouds it – is simply a string of
disconnected incidents. There is no continuity. Or rather, there is none
of the continuity of purposes and cross-purposes, developments and
declines, ambitions and differences which make history. When one
man goes, there is no one to take up the thread where he left off. The
blanket of the dark hides each group of climbers from its neighbours,
muffles up a thousand deeds of valour, and almost entirely prevents
the existence of dangerous rivalry. The undergraduate population
changes too frequently for roof-climbers to form an organized body.

Another reason for the lack of continuity is the absence of spurs
to ambition beyond a certain point. Mountaineers have always some
bigger mountain they hope to climb, some steeper rock-face they hope

to assault. But in Cambridge, with the exception of several dangerous or difficult buildings which few climbers attempt, there is no graded list of climbs, no classification of climbs according to their degree of severity. Thus, after he has done a number of difficult climbs a man feels he has reached a stage where he is no longer advancing, and he has no means to test himself by standard comparisons.

Again, the lack of written records makes a history of past roof-climbing impossible. Some records doubtless exist, in diaries or in log-books kept by individuals and by ephemeral night climbing societies. But the written word, where it exists, is kept hidden away, and so contributes nothing for the benefit of future generations. Practically the only exception is the *Roof-Climber's Guide to Trinity*, published anonymously many years ago, which has helped many an errant wayfarer in search of novelty over the less-known routes of Trinity. Descriptions of past adventures serve little purpose, save as anecdotes, but there is plenty of scope for descriptions and classifications to help future climbers.

This absence of literature on the subject can be easily understood. The college authorities, acting presumably on purely humanitarian motives, have set their official faces against roof-climbing, and no one would have it otherwise. It may lop off many a would-be climber who cannot risk being sent down, and keep many an adventurous spirit from the roof-tops, drain-pipes and chimneys, but this official disapproval is the sap which gives roof-climbing its sweetness. Without it, it would tend to deteriorate into a set of gymnastic exercises. Modesty drives the roof-climber to operate by night; the proctorial frown makes him an outlaw. And outlaws keep no histories.

For outlaw he is, and unless he take the common precautions of outlawry there will be trouble. He must dodge the proctors, with their attendant evil the bulldogs, on their nightly prowl round the streets of Cambridge. If he inadvertently clatters a stone or slate, he must evade the watchful eye of the college porter, standing near his lodge or walking round the college. When climbing near a road, he must know the policeman on the beat or the times when he is likely to pass.

It is surprising, on a roof, how little is needed to betray the position of the climber, or how much noise may be made with impunity. A loud, bold sound emanating from the darkness is difficult to locate, and is apt to pass unnoticed, while a low, scratching sound will arouse suspicion. Some years ago, a length of tarry string, falling with a small, smacking sound, caused a policeman to flash his torch upwards, and nearly betrayed the position of a party of four climbers on the roof of King's Chapel. More recently climbers at the top of two pinnacles on the same building were shouting across to each other, and, though many people may have heard them, they never felt in danger of detection. It is the soft, half-stifled sounds that are dangerous.

And the outlaw, if discovered on a roof, feels himself in a tight position, for he may not be able to descend without placing himself in the hands of authority. On most buildings there are alternative ways of descent, some of which are inaccessible to the pursuers, but the sensation of being trapped is not pleasant. The possibility of being heard or seen must very frequently be in the mind of the roof-climber, yet such is the protection afforded by night that the present writer only knows two who were ever caught.* Many have had narrow escapes, thrills that are seldom told save to intimate friends on rare occasions. The dismay felt by a climber descending a drain-pipe outside a college, with a porter inside shouting "Police!" at the top of his voice, is an emotion

---

* For "two" read "ten", and thereby hang a few tales to be told below.

never to be forgotten. Yet such an incident is recorded in a log-book now in the keeping of a respectable don of Cambridge.

Incidents of this sort occasionally happen, but they are rare; the exception rather than the rule. For the only people who are on the alert to detect roof-climbing really are the porters. The weary policeman trudging round his beat is usually a friendly fellow, as unwilling as the climbers to break the peace of the night. If they meet him on their way home, most climbers treat him as a confidant, tell him what they have done and swap stories with him. And if no damage has been done – as it never is – all will be well. The Robert is a friend.

The dons also give no trouble. A clumsy party sometimes causes a petulant old head to come to a window to see what all the clatter is about, but that is all. Even then he probably thinks of it, not as a heinous offence, but merely as an exhibition of bad manners to wake him up.

The younger dons, indeed, are often roof-climbers themselves. Out of a bare score whom the writer knows, four are active roof-climbers, and he knows of another four who have each reached the top of King's Chapel, usually reckoned the biggest climb in Cambridge. In fact, if you tactfully broach the subject to your supervisor, he may be able to help you considerably. And if you are very fortunate, he may even lead a midnight expedition in person. But like a naughty monk who slips out of the monastery after bed-time, he prefers the matter to be concealed from his colleagues. It is only the official side of authority which disapproves of roof-climbing.

Let no man think, however, that because many of the High Table are sympathetic, the punishment of offenders will be any the less if they are caught. Everyone knows the rules, and must play fair.

And so the game continues, unobtrusively, with each player igno-rant of the identity of most of his fellow enthusiasts. If they are good climbers, you will not often see them on buildings, but sometimes they are there. You may meet them in the early hours, or soon after sunset, padding along the streets in gym-shoes and old clothes. Perhaps, standing motionless in a dark doorway, they will startle you as you pass, as they study some building which they are about to climb. Or, capless and gownless, one of them may speed past you on his feet, pursued by a relentless and athletic anachronism in a top-hat, the proctor's bulldog.

There are numbers of them about, but you will seldom see them. They seldom even see each other. As furtively as the bats of twilight, they shun the eyes of the world, going on their mysterious journeys and retiring as quietly as they set out. Out of the darkness they come, in darkness they remain and into darkness they go, with most of their epics unrecorded and forgotten. Every college has its night climbers, yet contemporaries in the same college will often go through their university careers without discovering each other.

Most of them belong to no mountaineering club, and many of the regular mountaineers are not roof-climbers. Once a roof-climber called on the then President of the C.U. Mountaineering Club and asked him to participate in a particularly difficult climb. He was politely informed: "I am not a cat burglar". This is the attitude taken up by many mountain-climbers. Until they have tried themselves on buildings, they assume roof-climbing to be as straightforward as a rope in a gymnasium, a travesty in all ways of the true sport. Another Cambridge mountaineer with a fast-growing reputation – a freshman aged nineteen – refused to join us, saying that "he climbed only to find solitude". What he expected to find on the roof-tops we had not the heart to ask.

On the other hand, the greatest roof-climber we know has never climbed a mountain. The two sports are quite distinct, appealing to

5

the same instincts without helping or interfering with each other. And while mountaineers are counted by the tens of thousands, roof-climbers could scarcely be mustered by the dozen. Like characters from Buchan crossing a Scottish moor on a stormy night, they are silent and solitary, mysterious and unknown except to their own circle, preferring to live their own epics to reading those of others.

CHAPTER TWO

On Climbing In

"Come, thick night,
And pall thee in the dunnest smoke of hell,
That heaven peep not through the blanket of the dark,
To cry 'Hold, hold'"

Macbeth, slightly adapted

EVERY ROOF-CLIMBER in Cambridge probably started on his evil course in the same way, namely, by climbing into college.

The monastic seclusion into which a college draws itself at night begins at ten o'clock, when the gates are closed. At midnight the porter goes to bed, and no one may enter without a previous late leave from the proper source, dean or tutor. This is granted grudgingly, and is apt to be refused. A man who asks for it repeatedly feels an official coolness gazing askance at him. And even for coming back between the hours of ten and twelve he is fined a few pence, the exact sum varying from college to college.

Thus, whether to save gate-money or to remain a blue-eyed boy with his college dean, many an undergraduate sooner or later finds himself looking for an inconspicuous mode of entry into college. Why pain the dean, he argues to himself; why rouse the porter from his snores? And forgetting all the good advice of his youth, the tyro becomes naughty, and studies the problem of climbing in.

Now comes his first difficulty. He finds that the authorities have anticipated his naughtiness and barred the ground-floor windows. Wandering round the college he finds that the obvious ways are guarded by revolving spikes, which are apt to spin under the drunkard's foot and drive into his thigh. Every year there are a number of minor accidents of this sort in Cambridge, and there are seasoned roof-climbers who cannot negotiate spikes.

So he wanders round, trying a side door here, testing a bar there, wondering whether he can squeeze round some spikes, or surveying longingly an easy drain-pipe running up past a first-floor window.* Usually he has been told of an easy way in – "An absolute cinch, any fool can do it" – but when the time comes he finds it somewhat fearsome. Twelve feet of easy drain-pipe is not so easy when he is eight feet from the ground; stepping over spikes is an operation requiring flexibility of joints and great delicacy of balance. He hesitates, and keeps looking round to see if a proctor is coming to catch him and send him down from Cambridge to his weeping parents.

At last, the ordeal ended, he finds himself in college, not quite sure whether to be proud or ashamed of himself. After the first few minutes, sure that he is safe, he is no longer doubtful, and he will often climb in again. He has had his first taste of night climbing.

Night climbing is a better term to describe the sport it represents than roof-climbing. For the latter suggests a long ramble between banks

---

* A certain friend of ours, wanting to climb into St John's and knowing no easy way, found his way up to the roof and began to test skylights and trap-doors. At last he found one which would open and lowered himself down to arm's length. Not being able to see what was below him, he dropped and trusted to luck. A moment later an unfortunate man, sleeping immediately beneath the trapdoor, was awakened by two feet carrying thirteen stone driving into his side.

Spikes. The three rows all revolve.

of sloping slates, and peering in awe over the edge of a building whose roof one reaches by a trap-door. And many men believe it to consist of this. In point of fact, all night climbing takes place on the face of buildings, and on the spires and towers above the roof-tops. To enter college by an easy but uncountenanced way is the first step to night climbing, though it could seldom be called roof-climbing.

By far the greater number of undergraduates stop when they have found a satisfactory way of climbing in. It is the few, the handful of men in each college who are caught by the fascination of buildings by night, who become the night climbers.

How and why each man takes to the sport varies in each case. Perhaps a friend has persuaded him into it. Perhaps one of the occasional pictures which appear in the papers of a building crowned with a cap or gown has fired his imagination, and stirred him to emulation. Perhaps he is in one of those few colleges where a fair degree of climbing skill must be acquired before they can be entered at all. One man, locked out of his room late at night by a playful humorist, saw that by climbing a thirty-foot drain-pipe he could enter by the window, and so avoid waking the porter. He became an enthusiastic climber.

Many would-be beginners hesitate to start, because they think they would have no head for it. They manage to struggle into college, and because it may be difficult they assume that night climbing would be much more so. And so, perhaps, they confess to someone in their last term, "I always meant to do something like that myself, but somehow did nothing about it".

The best answer to this complaint is: Do something about it, now. There must be hundreds of men throughout the university who feel that it is a sport they would like, and who lose it only through failure to make a start. To such men, to anyone who feels even a slight urge to go

Over the railings to the Old Library.

out climbing, it cannot be too often repeated; start now. Do something definite; make arrangements to go out on the first fine night. By fine is meant any night when it is not raining; for climbs exposed to view an overcast night is best. Find, if possible, a man with experience, however little, of night climbing, and ask him to take you out. If you know of none, then take another beginner like yourself, and start together. You will be surprised how easy it can be.

The fear of heights is the easiest of all fears to cure, though one of the most troublesome while it exists. Giddiness, the mental paralysis which makes its victims unable to do simple things when there is a drop below them, blind fear of heights, all can be cured in two or three outings, starting with easy climbs and small heights.

The root of the trouble lies usually in the mistaken attitude of the beginner. Instead of looking at an easy scramble close to the ground and thinking "I could do that", he looks at some forbidding vertical wall which he knows has been climbed, and feels "I could never do that". When told that an impossible-looking building is a field for climbers, he is apt to feel, like a child watching a conjurer, that there is magic in it and it is not for him. So he shies, and perhaps never makes a start.

The climber himself is too often responsible for driving away possible recruits. For climbers are a boastful fraternity, very apt to magnify their minor deeds into heroic achievements and the longer climbs into epics. The seasoned veteran loves to point smugly at a building and say "We went up that last night". The way he says it and the sight of the building are enough to discourage all but the stoutest-hearted. If the hearer could see the route up, hand by hand and step by step, he might realize that it was not so very difficult after all.

In fact, it is a fairly safe rule to consider any climb as being considerably easier than it is described by the climber. Beginners, not in a position to call the bluff, may take too seriously what is only meant as an armchair gesture. Let the would-be beginner console himself with the thought that, provided he sincerely wishes to climb, it is a sport which can be mastered more quickly than any other. The expert who talks so largely is no superman. Half a dozen outings should bring the novice up to a fair standard, and the "head for heights" will come very rapidly after the first night.

Anyone can test his own head for himself. If he can lean out of a window thirty feet from the ground without feeling any fear or discomfort, he has a head which can become trained to climbing. If he can crouch on the outside of the window-sill, holding on to the inside of the window, and still feel no uneasiness, he will make good progress.

Not very severe tests? Maybe not, but many who are now good climbers could not at one stage in their lives have passed the second test without some feeling of trepidation.

The physical qualifications are such as would be passed by nineteen people out of twenty, and even this is probably a low estimate. A moderate degree of fitness is advisable, but the type of man who wants to climb is not likely to have become flabby in his undergraduate days. Strength of arm is more important in roof-climbing than in mountain-climbing. Yet it is surprising how little need be used. A man who can pull on a horizontal bar until his chin is level with his hands should be able to manage the severest climbs. The writer has never yet heard of a climb where a man had to pull himself up with one arm, and it is extremely rarely that he has to pull himself up with his arms without using his legs.

What is usually called a "sense of balance", but should more properly be called the art of balancing, is an attribute which grows rapidly with experience, and is closely linked with the "head for heights".

Thus the qualifications, mental and physical, are not severe. Yet beginners sometimes complain that they are not losing their fear of heights, even after two or three outings. This is because they are starting on too difficult climbs.

A normal man experiences fear when he feels that he is in danger. Even an expert climber feels fear on rare occasions when something goes wrong. Much more so will the novice feel it if the climb is too difficult for him. Without the confidence of knowing exactly what to do, he has the thought of a fall at the back or the front of his mind, and unless he be made of exceptionally stern stuff his climbing will become temporarily inefficient. Secured by a rope on the same climb, he will probably climb confidently and without fear.

It is the conquest of this fear that adds half the charm to climbing. However good the climber, there are always climbs just beyond his scope, frightening him until he has conquered them, and himself. Then there is another. Just a shade harder, coaxing, taunting, bullying him until he has made a successful ascent up its defiant length. It is only by seeing how easy have become his early efforts that a climber realizes how he has progressed. He still feels the same thrills, the same excitements as when he started, and as he continues to conquer his fear, greater difficulties step forward to challenge him. And it is a challenge that he must accept if he would continue to go forward, for he may not stand still. A single failure weakens for future occasions the will to reach the top; every success is a gain in confidence.

There may be men who have never known this fear, or have exterminated it by will-power or relentless self-discipline. If there be such men, they must climb as a child skips, for sheer ecstatic enjoyment. For, to the enthusiast, there is a tremendous pleasure to be found even in doing a climb well within his scope, for the fun of doing it. The charm of night climbing is of a kind that is not to be found elsewhere.

CHAPTER THREE

For Beginners Only

"Silence is a friend that will never betray"

Confucius

H AVING DECIDED to make a start, the beginner will want a few
questions answered before he sets out. First and foremost,
he wants to know what to wear.

Any old coat will serve for climbing. A rough coat, however, is apt
to be troublesome in a chimney, since it catches on the rough stone
behind the climber's back, and prevents him from sliding up or down.
In an easy chimney this does not matter, but in an awkward chimney it can make a very troublesome difference. In such a situation a
smooth, golfing jacket is to be preferred, but there are few places in
Cambridge where the difference is appreciable, and the beginner is
not likely to find them on his first time out.

Long trousers are better than shorts. The knees and the finger-
knuckles are the most valuable parts of the night climber, and the long
trousers will save him from many a scratch or graze. It is wise to give
the ends an extra turn-up, or he may catch his toe or heel in his trousers
at a moment when he least wants his attention to be distracted. The
slight extra feeling of freedom which shorts give is not worth their

attendant penalty of scratched knees.

Rubber shoes complete the necessary clothing. Black gum-shoes, which are cheap, are not conspicuous, and every climber who intends to go out often should buy a pair. Rare roof-climbers who are also mountain-climbers prefer to climb in nailed boots, but these are not to be recommended. Rubbers are much better on a dry night, and if a shower causes them to lose their grip it is best to come down and go home. In the wet, bare feet grip better than rubbers, and it is not painful to climb bare-footed. As an experiment, a certain thick-skinned enthusiast climbed for two months in bare feet before deciding that he preferred rubbers. Even today, he prefers bare feet to boots on mountains. And on Cambridge buildings, boots scratch and damage the stone-work, which is not consistent with the night climber's ideal of leaving no trace where he has been.

The use of the rope in climbing is a controversial matter. A rope is not necessary, but is an asset. There is a strong tendency to regard the rope as the hallmark of the expert climber. It is nothing of the kind. It should be regarded as an additional safeguard, only to be used in places which the climbers find difficult or dangerous.

With a rope many climbs can be undertaken in Cambridge which would be unwise or impossible without one. In such cases, the rope can usually be taken up by an easier way, and lowered down the difficult climb from above. This is a practice to be strongly discouraged, and we know of only one occasion on which it has been indulged in. It is the writer's opinion that no climb should be attempted on a rope which the climber would be incapable of achieving unroped. An experienced climber can lead a novice up difficult places, but climbs should not be attempted where none of the party is willing or able to manage the climb without the help of a rope from above.

The rope itself should be of the best obtainable quality, the proper Alpine hemp, which is distinguishable by the three red strands, visible at the ends, which run down as a sort of core inside. The longer the rope, up to a hundred feet or more, the better it is. Forty feet is too short for many Cambridge climbs, allowing for the fact that both climbers have it tied round themselves, and the top climber must try to belay the rope round the nearest available anchorage.

A piece of cord, ten or twenty feet long, is also sometimes useful. For climbing or descending, the rope should be over the climber's waist – there is a special knot for it – and the surplus coils are carried on his shoulders by the second man. He pays them out as the leader advances, taking care never to jerk the rope tight. It is not wise to have three men on a rope in Cambridge. As most of the climbing is vertical, the leader should be off the pitch before the next man starts. This is very important. If the climb is severe, the leader can take a ball of string with which to haul up the rope, thus freeing himself of its drag. This is more satisfactory than carrying the whole rope coiled on his shoulder.

The top man, if he can find no anchorage, should draw the rope sharply over the angle of the roof or parapet on which he is standing. Even if it be less than a right angle, the stone-work will take a good proportion of the weight, so that the leader can usually hold the rope comfortably with one hand. If he continually draws the rope in, there will be no jerk should the second climber slip.

A strong weight of opinion exists that the use of the rope is bad on all but the most severe climbs, as it has a bad moral effect. It kills confidence. The leader, says this school, learns to doubt the ability of his party to follow him up without a rope. Those who are roped up come to depend upon the sense of security it gives them and, however good they may be, they tend to lose their self-reliance.

17

Certain it is that a climb takes much longer when the party is roped. Furthermore, a rope creates an atmosphere of gravity which is apt to make a man climb more slowly. Some climbers, at least, find that they climb better unroped than otherwise. Alone, a man trusts himself – there is no alternative – and acts accordingly. On a rope there is apt to be the feeling of being supported by a better man, and this does not increase self-reliance. After being roped up, even if he does not slip – as he never does – a man is inclined to think: "I could never have done it without a rope". Unroped, he would have done it. And his moral fibre would have been strengthened instead of weakened.

A small but select school stands for the use of the rope on all possible occasions. Being roped, say they, relieves a climber of any immediate fear, and enables him to find for himself how easy it is. It is fear which impedes a climber's freedom of action, and on a rope he could do with confidence what he would not otherwise dare do.

These are the two schools of thought, and the beginner must decide between them. The truth probably lies half-way between. If he compromise, he will be able to test and increase his ability while roped to a leader, and develop his self-reliance unroped. Let him beware, however, against the insidiousness of the roping habit. Better by far never to rope at all than to rope for easy climbs. The writer is convinced that over-roping, like drug-taking, weakens the subject for future occasions. But used sparingly the rope has the benediction of most climbers. It can conveniently be concealed in a gown slung over the arm, or under the coat if there are proctors about.

Two is the ideal number for climbing. Solitary climbers are sometimes met with on mountains, but in Cambridge they must be very exceptional; we have only known one serious roof-climber who preferred to go out alone. Three is a possible number, but is more cumbrous, slower and more noisy. And since no chain is stronger than its weakest link, the greater the number the less venturesome is likely to be the party. Two, climbing regularly together, get to know each other's strength and weaknesses. However, the matter is not very important, and will solve itself.

When to climb is equally unimportant. Summer nights are short and sweet, but are marred by the thought of the Tripos and impending damnation. And no time of the year is too cold. A party of four climbers, in February, were exposed to a howling east wind for over two hours on a roof with the temperature several degrees below freezing. They record that they felt no cold, although they wore no gloves, and only two men could climb at once. The excitement and the occasional exercise kept them warm.

Whatever the time of year, however, it must be a fine night. Night climbing is no fun in the rain, and the most ardent enthusiast can find plenty of fine nights for his purpose.

The state of the moon has a considerable influence on night climbing. Other things being equal, most climbers probably prefer to climb under the blaze of a full moon. The majority of climbs are too exposed for this, except well after midnight, when the climber can relax some of his precautions against discovery.

No night is too dark for climbing. It is surprising how much can be seen on the darkest of nights, and while the climber can be concealed from observation he can see all the handholds and footholds around him. A formidable exception to this generalization is the Drain-pipe Chimney on the outer west wall of St John's, of which more later. Suffice it to say at present that this chimney must be the darkest spot in Cambridge.

The ideal time of night is between midnight and 2 a.m. The proctors are off the streets, and if an irate don sends for the porters they must dress, by the end of which time the climbers should be well away. And bed by two-thirty once a week will not hurt even a man in training.

For a secluded climb passing close to a don's window, a very good time in the winter is between seven-thirty and eight o'clock, when Hall dinner is being served for the High Table. The John's Drain-pipe Chimney, for instance, or the Chetwynd Chimney in King's, both of which run through a nest of dons, could very well be done at this time. Both of these chimneys are close to an easy way out of college, however, so the climber has little to worry him.

The beginner, straining at the leash, is probably wondering where to start, what climbs to do first. For this reason, there was a strong temptation to grade every climb in this book as easy, moderate, difficult, severe, or very severe. Fortunately, wiser counsel prevailed. A few climbers may be disappointed at not having the standard of their achievements labelled for them, but they can do this for themselves. Night climbing is not a competitive sport.

What appears easy to one climber appears difficult to another and *vice versa*. Climbers of equal calibre often disagree radically as to the degree of difficulty of a particular climb. What is difficult to a beginner may become easy to him in a month's time, and what would be classed "difficult" is merely two degrees harder than "easy". The climber, even an absolute novice, may find climbs well within his scope from which he might have been discouraged by the forbidding sound of the classification. A man known to the writer, by no means an expert climber, made his first salutation to the roof-tops leading up a severe climb. Classifications are more of a deterrent than a help.

Finally a word about sobriety. By far the greater number of men climb sober, and for an expert climber it is unquestionably better to do so. One man has told the writer that he notices a deterioration in his climbing after a single glass of beer. Another would never climb unless he was three-parts drunk, however, and was then extremely efficient. Whether drink improves climbing or causes it to deteriorate depends upon the character and constitution of each particular man. Where it gives "Dutch courage" without impairing muscular control, it may send a moderate climber soaring up places that defy the sober expert. Under the influence of alcohol, a man with an object in view often acquires an accentuated power of concentration upon that one object. And if that object be climbing, he will climb brilliantly. Many men have noticed that it is easier to climb into college while intoxicated, and the same applies sometimes to serious climbing.

Nevertheless, it is dangerous to attempt a serious climb while drunk or under the influence of drink. For the climber may "sober up" at the crucial point of the climb and lose his "Dutch courage". And while on one occasion drink may improve the standard of climbing, the next night it may have precisely the opposite effect.

Besides, a climber is continually conquering his fear, and enjoys doing so. If he allows drink to do this for him, is it not a confession that he cannot do so alone? It may at first need more courage to do an easy climb while sober than a difficult climb while drunk, but then the lesser climb is the greater achievement.

CHAPTER FOUR

Drain-pipes

"Very like a whale"

Hamlet

CAMBRIDGE CLIMBING falls very largely into two categories: drain-pipe and chimney. Good climbs up stone faces can be found in plenty for those who want them, but every night climber should be able to climb a drain-pipe if necessary. The drain-pipe is the most urgent thing to be mastered by the beginner. With drain-pipe technique in his hands and knees, he will have the confidence to tackle any climb in Cambridge, for, in our opinion, it is the hardest part of the art to learn.

To those who are unfamiliar with drain-pipes, it might seem that one is as good as another. To the climber each pipe has its own individuality. It may be loose, or tightly clamped to the wall. It may touch the wall, or stand half an inch out so that there is finger-room behind. It may be as thin as a man's wrist or as thick as his thigh; the former is better for hand-grip, the latter for knee-grip. The surface of the wall may be smooth, or it may be rough, offering a certain amount of friction-hold for the feet. Sometimes the pipe is bound at intervals with iron, sometimes not. It may go past window-ledges which serve as

Drain-pipe technique.

On the Engineering Labs.

resting-places every fifteen feet, or it may be fixed to a bare wall. Sometimes it is in a corner, or better still, a foot or two away from a corner. It may be near a street light, or in a place where only the moon and the stars reveal the man who is climbing. It may go right to the top, or it may end a few feet short of the roof.

Consider, for instance, those pipes on the face of Gonville and Caius in Trinity Street. They are forty feet high, yet would seem to have been installed especially for climbers, easier than many pipes half their height.

To begin with, they are firmly clamped to the wall. The wall is smooth and the pipes so rigid that the climber knows he can trust every foot- and hand-hold. Each pipe is bound by steel bands at alternate intervals of about five and three feet, which protrude about three-quarters of an inch from the pipe. They would provide narrow but adequate foot-holds, and check all tendency of the hands to slip down the smooth pipe.

In addition, there are horizontal ledges running along the building at convenient intervals, and windows with ornamental stone-work close to most of the pipes. Their exposed position in an important street keeps most climbers away from them, but after midnight they are fairly safe, and appear to offer a delightful climb on to the roof of Caius. Yet in the climb of the face of Caius they are practically useless, for one reason. There is no finger-room behind them.

On the other hand, consider those pipes in the New Court of St John's, over the river. Much more exposed-looking than those of Caius, with no ornamental stone-work to help, there are nevertheless one or two of them which can be climbed direct because there is finger-room behind. We know of no-one who has climbed any of the pipes on the outer north wall of the same court. They are the most forbidding pipes in Cambridge.

St John's, Drain-pipe Chimney.

Nearly seventy feet in height, they run up a smooth wall, away from any windows or ornamental stone-work. They are affixed to the wall with a minimum number of clamps, and instead of steel bindings every few feet there is a continuous length of smooth pipe. Most repelling feature of all, they run in places so close to the wall that there is no finger-room behind. A hunchback dwarf would not enjoy climbing them, and we doubt if they are possible. However, if any hero wish to attempt one of them, he had best have a rope lowered from the roof, which can be reached by two or three ways. It would be a severe pull on the arms, and there is no possible resting-place *en route*.

Then look at the drain-pipes on either side from the roof to the tower of the Great Gate of Trinity, and shudder again. They run up a bare brick wall and stop four feet short of the battlements. But they are sometimes climbed, and to his surprise the climber finds them quite easy.

Some pipes in Cambridge are square or rectangular, instead of round. These are no good for climbing. They are usually clamped close to the wall, and are apt to be loose. They offer no pull towards the wall, so that the climber must counter the tendency to fall away from them. So much for the anatomy of drain-pipes.

There are two different ways of climbing a drain-pipe. The natural method is to have the whole body away from the wall, except the hands and toes. The feet push the body outwards and upwards against the wall, while the hands pull inwards and upwards on the pipe. Thus the climber goes up like a monkey on a rope, hand over hand, and feet walking up the wall.

This method has speed in its favour, but cannot always be used. It is only possible when there is finger-room behind for the whole length of the pipe. It tends to pull a loose pipe away from the wall, especially as the push from the legs has to be counteracted. It imposes a continual strain on the climber's arms when there are no other holds.

The other way is to keep as close to the wall as possible. On a pitch where there is no hold for the hands or feet the climber must move caterpillar-wise, gripping tightly with his knees and with the insteps of his feet also pressing against the pipe. Since he must rely upon his arms as well as his legs for such pitches, it is best to choose the easier pipes, where there are supplementary holds.

Holding on to a vertical pipe is more tiring than holding on to a horizontal grip. The pipe only offers a friction hold, which is harder to retain than a hold on to a ledge of horizontal projection. For this reason every possible additional hold should be used. And where a good foothold is found, it will take the strain off the arms for a much-needed relief. Clamps, steel bindings, ornamental ledges and window-ledges, flanges over the top of windows – everything should be used.

Most men find drain-pipes the easiest part of Cambridge, and those of us who do not are accused of "personal bias". The beginner should nevertheless acclimatize himself slowly, starting on easy pipes with an abundance of external holds. If he should feel any qualms when half-way up, there is one thought which should console him. It is much easier to come down than to go up a drain-pipe.

For in going up, the heavy work is thrown upon the arms. In coming down he can to a large extent spare them, sliding down slowly with his knees, and using his hands only to keep his body from falling away from the wall. He will never go very far before a clamp or steel binding will enable him to rest, and where there are plenty of holds he should go down in bounds, from hold to hold.

This certain feeling that he can get down will encourage a climber to go on even when the conviction sears his soul that he does not like drain-pipes. Knowing that a safe route down to earth lies below him, he will pluck up courage to "try the next bit", and so reach the top.

Although drain-pipes are an essential part of night climbing, they are not usually an end in themselves, but only a means to an end. Certain pipes, because of their position in relation to the surrounding stone-work, offer interesting climbing in themselves, but there are not many of them. Very few night climbers have ever ascended a thirty-foot pipe on the exposed face of a building. A few enthusiasts swarm up every pipe they see, for its own sake, but they are not necessarily good climbers. They are gymnasts.

CHAPTER FIVE

On Chimneys

"He hath inclosed my ways with hewn stone"
Lamentations, iii. 9

IN CLIMBING parlance a chimney is a fissure between two walls,
in which the climber has his back against one wall and his feet
against the other. By exerting pressure with his legs he creates
sufficient friction to prevent himself from slipping, even if there are
no hand-holds. In a suitable chimney between two vertical walls it
is possible to climb with the arms crossed, for they are not essential.
In other chimneys, especially those that are narrow, the hands must
supplement the chimneying action.

Chimneys vary as much as drain-pipes. But to the climber (as
opposed to the gymnast) they offer better climbing, because more can
be entrusted to the legs. They pertain to mountains as well as to buildings, unlike drain-pipes, and so are known to mountaineers as well as
to night climbers. George Abraham, veteran mountaineer, says in one
of his books that a good climber is known, not by the way he uses his
hands, but by the way he uses his feet. This is especially so in chimneys.
Where the bad climber uses a hand-pull, the expert thrusts himself up
with his legs. And since the legs can support the body without becoming

tired, chimneying is reckoned the least exhausting form of climbing.

Chimney-climbing in Cambridge is both more severe and at the same time more straightforward than on mountains. Paradoxical as it may sound, this statement can be easily explained.

All buildings being vertical, the chimneys on their faces must perforce be vertical also. Some mountains have vertical faces, and vertical cracks in their sides, yet by far the greater number of chimneys that are climbed are sloping. And a sloping chimney is apt to be less fearsome.

Furthermore, mountains have not been smoothed out by the touch of the stone-mason. The inequalities of the rock provide knobs and cavities which give a greater purchase to the sole of the foot, and handholds where they are needed. Mountain chimneys offer many facilities which the night climber must do without.

On the other hand, there are points in favour of the Cambridge chimneys. Though perpendicular, they are regular. On a mountain the chimneyist, working steadily upwards, may suddenly find himself in difficulties arising out of that very irregularity of the mountain which has been helping him. The walls may converge, or gradually widen apart; a boulder may be wedged in the chimney so as to obstruct the climber, or the rock may become crumbly and flake off. If the boot slips on a crumbling piece of rock in a chimney, woe betide the climber!

Cambridge offers none of these unexpected difficulties. The climber can study the chimney in daylight and note such peculiarities as may affect him. Even the leader can often be roped up if he will, and it is comforting to know exactly what lies ahead. The hand- and foot-holds, where they exist, can be trusted, and the climber prefers to know what he has to face, even if it be severe. The pitches are often difficult, but they are short, which makes them less formidable than if they occurred on a mountain in the course of a long day's climb.

By the Eagle Chimney, on to the roof of the Cloisters.

And now as to the method of climbing chimneys.

In the photograph of the climber in the chimney by St John's south gate, a typical chimneying position can be seen. The left leg is doubled beneath the body. The right is stretched out, with the toes of the foot pressing against the wall opposite. The hands, though stroking the wall affectionately, are doing no work. The body is just away from the wall, preparatory to moving up.

Although we have said that in an easy chimney the arms might be folded, they can be of some use for helping to push the body upwards. For this, place them on a level with the hips, slightly to each side of the body, palms towards the wall. Then leaning slightly forward, so as to avoid the friction of the wall, press the hands downwards while at the same time straightening the leg which is doubled beneath the body without allowing the foot to slip downwards. The body will rise.

Then, lean back firmly against the wall. Bring the foot from underneath you across to the opposite wall, above the other foot. Both feet are now on the opposite wall, one above the other. Bring the lower foot under the body, doubling the leg into a comfortable position for pushing upwards. You are now in the same position that you started from, except that the right leg instead of the left is beneath you, and the left on the wall opposite, where the right had been. And you are a foot or so higher. Repeat the process, and you will be exactly in the position you started from, only two moves higher.

In a chimney of suitable width this action can be repeated at fair speed. In the course of every move upwards, each foot is transferred from one wall to the other in a rhythmic action which is pleasant to watch. As long as he keeps his head, the climber can reach the top of the chimney by this means.

And where he can climb comfortably all the way by chimneying, the climber should beware of using extraneous hand- or foot-holds. They may enable him to climb quicker, but they may also throw him out of rhythm, unless he be an experienced chimneyist. There is a natural temptation to grab any hold he may see, or stand on any ledge he may be passing, but the wise chimney-climber will resist it.

A novice, surprised at the easiness of chimneying, is apt to get about twenty feet up and then, looking down and seeing nothing but smooth wall below him, to have an attack of the "willies". This is where a little self-reasoning will help. He knows that, as long as he continues to chimney correctly he will be safe, and if he keeps his head he will find no difficulty to worry him. It is best to chimney up and down small distances until the procedure becomes instinctive.

We said earlier in the chapter that chimneys vary as much as drain-pipes. They differ from the latter in that the action of chimneying can be used in places where the novice would not think of it, and would thus be unable to get up. For instance, the first overhang on the pinnacles of King's Chapel, twenty feet above the roof, has a height of five feet without hand-holds, and appears to be impossible. However, by chimneying between the pillar and the centre of the ornamental stone-work the climber can surmount the difficulty, and so with the second overhang, even more fearsome, on to the parapet.

Other Cambridge chimneys have their idiosyncrasies. The Old Library Chimney becomes narrow near the top, and the climber has to perform a gymnastic twist to bring his back on to the opposite wall. This would be practically impossible but for some projecting brick-ends which provide good hand-holds. The Chetwynd Chimney in King's is so narrow as to be back-and-knee rather than back-and-foot, and is blocked by two apparently insurmountable chockstones. To be successful the climber must leave the chimney for an adjacent window-ledge.

But the sun is setting. Enthusiasts will now make a tour of some of the interesting climbs of Cambridge, we hope in fact as well as by the fireside. There is no moon, the sky is cloudy and the barometer is high. It will be a fine night.

CHAPTER SIX

The Old Library

"Then I said unto them, what is the high place
Whereunto you go?"

Ezekiel xx. 29

T O THE man who would take up night climbing seriously, the
Old Library offers an ideal nursery. No dons or porters will
disturb his first clumsy attempts, no proctor who hears him
is likely to guess the source of the noise. He may pad about fearlessly
in his dark gym-shoes, and concentrate only on the climbing problems
before him. The absolute novice may let in the first gear on easy climbs,
and the advanced expert will still find work worthy of his efforts. The
only nocturnal inhabitant, the caretaker, lives in the south-west corner,
overlooking King's, and far removed from the climbing side. So if the
novice will come along with us, we will try to arouse his enthusiasm
and whet his appetite for further expeditions.

As we pass down Senate House Passage from King's Parade to
Trinity Hall, the Senate House on our left gives way to some iron railings, connecting it to the highest part of the Old Library. It is these
railings that we must cross.

Broad and pointed like a row of prehistoric javelins, they are

On the Old Library − up to the Saintless Niche.

nevertheless very blunt, and the novice may tackle them without fear of injury. If he should find them difficult, a press-up will help him. When the hands are level with the hips, he can raise a foot on to the narrow horizontal ribbon running nine inches from the top. Having got across, he may lower himself as best he will. The easiest place to cross is the side of the gate half-way along the railings, although it is under the full glare of a lamp-post. A projection sideways here makes the balance easy, whereas crossing the straight line of railings farther along is rather difficult. As he turns on the top of the railings, the Gate of Honour in Gonville and Caius shows itself within five yards of him, across the passage.

We are now on the scene of action. On the right is a large double doorway above which is written the word Biblioteca. A huge awning-ledge projects for about four feet above it, at a height of ten feet from the ground. Here Eager Egbert can try his first climb. This is to get on to the top of the awning ledge.

As a sheer feat of strength this is difficult, but it can be made easy by chimneying at the side as a help to the pull-up. With his head level with the ledge, the climber may remove both his hands to show that the body can be supported by chimneying along. Some iron bars on the window above give additional help, but the climber can go no farther than this ledge. If a novice can do this (and it is not difficult) he can become a good climber.

Immediately in front of us there is a drain-pipe, running from the ground to the roof, a height of between twenty-five and thirty feet. This is the Sunken Drain-pipe. Five yards to the right is a gap between two walls, running up past two windows. This is the Old Library Chimney. We will leave both of these for the moment and proceed to the far railings, by King's.

Passing along an archway with pillars on the left, we come to the high railings separating the Old Library from King's. Along the top is a row of revolving spikes, so that the railings cannot be climbed direct. This does not matter, for it is the building on which we want to climb, and not the spikes.

As seen in the photograph, the stone is slotted, but the slots are V-shaped, and sloping, so that they cannot be used as a ladder. Nevertheless, it is possible without much difficulty to get on to the ledge above the railings. It might be possible, but would be extremely unwise, to go higher, and in our opinion the roof could not be reached by this route. Even if a climber could get near the top (as he might, on a rope), he would be confronted with an insurmountable overhang. So let him go to the right, where a saintless niche confronts him. Here he may ensconce himself, and imagine for a few minutes that he is petrified, with a stony halo round his head.

A Kingsman will observe that this offers an illicit method of entry into his college. Furthermore, it is a genteel way which he can use without soiling his knees and elbows, should he be in evening dress. We give it without compunction, because there are half a dozen easier ways.

Ten yards along to the right there is another niche, also saintless, which can be reached from the ground. This is a difficult bit of climbing, requiring a delicate balance. Starting immediately under the niche, one must make use of the archway on the right, with an underhand grip. This helps to prevent one from falling outwards. The niche sinks deep into the wall, so that having reached it one may rest in comfort.

An exactly similar niche, except that every hand-grip is reversed, is to be found at the other end of the pillars. By climbing up to each of these niches in succession a climber may, if he wish, compare the efficiency of his right side with that of his left. The difference may astonish him.

Old Library Chimney from below.

We will now go up to the roof.

There are two routes up, both of which will be severe to a novice. These are the Sunken Drain-pipe and the Old Library Chimney. We will take the latter first. It is to be found twenty yards from the Senate House Passage railings, on the right. The climber must face south, as the windows on the south side come too close to the side wall to leave room for the climber's body. On the north side a buttress leaves a recess into which a man's body fits nicely. The chimney is too broad for comfort, and a very short man might find it impossible to reach the opposite wall, with his feet flapping disconsolately in space like an elephant's uvula.

The second window comes very close indeed to the wall, and the feet must keep to a vertical strip of stone only three inches wide. Proceeding indomitably upwards, we bump our head a nasty crack and pause to think.

Old Library Chimney – the headless man.

The recess between the buttress and the wall suddenly ceases to exist. From being too broad, the chimney becomes too narrow.

Some convenient brick-ends projecting from the wall above make further progress possible. To be able to make use of them we must have our back against the opposite wall. Turning round in a chimney is not easy, but holding on to a brick-end with one hand we can make a gymnastic twist, and from then onwards the climb is easy.* With the brick-ends before us, we can do the last six or seven feet up to the roof behind us in comfort.

Now down again, to the Sunken Drain-pipe. This offers a climb which even in Cambridge is unique. Being sunk, as the photograph shows, between a projecting wall and a buttress, it prevents the climber

---

* It is possible to get up without turning round, by using the flange above the window for the feet. It is difficult.

Sunken Drain-pipe – lower half.

Sunken Drain-pipe – upper half. It was on this part of the pipe
that disaster nearly occurred to one of our party.

from getting both feet on it at once. He must use the slotted stone-work on the left. The pipe is slightly farther away from the buttress than from the left wall, and leaves just enough room to wedge the right foot. The right hand can just get a grip behind the pipe.

The left foot is stretched right out to the side, to the edge of the projecting blocks of stone. Getting it as high as possible, press hard on it, at the same time shoving hard with the right foot, pulling outwards with the right arm, and to the right with the left hand against the edge eighteen inches away. It looks fiendishly severe but is actually quite easy.

For the last ten or twelve feet the recess widens, and it is possible to get both feet beside the pipe. The stone is rough, and for this short distance you can walk straight up. There is a loose corner-stone at the top of which a panting novice must beware; it is quite easy to tell which it is and to avoid it.

The climber who has reached the roof by these two methods need consider himself a novice no longer.

A few lines above a sentence starts, "There is a loose corner-stone". For "is" read "was", and we will explain why the tense has been changed.

After we first wrote this chapter, five climbers went up to obtain a photograph of the Tottering Tower. Two were already on the roof, two were on the pipe ten feet apart (the upper man almost on the roof) and the writer nearing the top of the chimney on the right. The upper man on the pipe, to rest for a few moments before the final pull up, placed his left elbow on the corner of the ledge on the left. We had forgotten to warn him, and he said it looked quite safe. Although he exerted little pressure, a whole length of the ledge, eighteen inches long, and weighing some thirty or forty pounds, broke off and fell.

Now comes the extraordinary part of the tale. The climber below was holding on to the pipe with both hands at the same level, waiting for the man above to leave his way clear. The stone, falling across his arms, cut a gash through his tweed coat and shirt, and made a nasty cut in his arm, besides grazing his head *en route*. But his two elbows acted as a spring, taking the greater part of the shock, and after laying the stone on the ledge on his left, the climber was able to complete the climb. Had we taken our own advice in a previous chapter never to have two climbers on a pitch at the same time, this flirtation with calamity could never have happened.

The lower climber afterwards told us that he was not frightened by the stone falling. What he found unpleasant was looking up a few moments before, when he saw a chink of light between the ledge and the wall, and knew that the stone was about to fall. His suspense was prolonged for a second or two by the upper climber holding on to the stone until his strength gave out.

The upper climber was slightly shaken by this incident. He did not allow it to affect his climbing, but several times in the next night or two he looked thoughtful. On the way down he had already lowered himself over the edge when his hold on the roof stiffened. He came up again and said the top of the pipe had broken.

At the time this seemed almost as serious as the previous incident. Had he released his hold on the roof, it seemed he must have fallen. The writer, who had witnessed the first episode, began to wonder whether the luck had turned, and experienced some nasty sensations. They came down the chimney and the others, who had gone down the pipe, said the bowl was loose but the pipe safe. The man with the gashed sleeve was entirely unmoved, and would hardly be persuaded to keep the stone as a memento. And now back to the Sunken Drain-pipe.

About fifteen feet up there are two ledges, three feet apart. The upper one is three or four inches broad, and inclined to be crumbly. The lower one is only an inch or two broad, but perfectly safe. These two ledges are known as the Old Library Traverse. We have never been the whole way along (which extends as far as King's) but it is a recognized climb. When moving the hands along the upper ledge, slide them along and never take either hand completely away.

There is a third route, as far as we know not yet exploited, whereby the roof could be reached from the ground. This is between Trinity Hall and the north gate of King's, on the left as one faces south.

In a recess between a rounded wall and a bay window, two pipes run upwards to the roof. After prolonged study from the ground we decided it was a possible climb and magnanimously left it for future generations to conquer. It is a height of forty to fifty feet, and we cannot say whether it would prove easy or very severe.

Seen from the top it looks severe. Further, the last stretch of pipe rattles, although it seems safe enough. A couple of climbers, prowling round the roof, decided to have nothing to do with it.

Once the roof is reached, the Old Library offers one further climb. All the different roof-levels are connected with iron ladders, and it is possible to wander at will in all directions. There is no particular need for silence, but remember the caretaker in the south-west corner.

The climb which remains to be done is that needle-shaped erection on the west side, which we have named the O'Hara Pinnacle or Tottering Tower. The climber in the photograph will now take the pen.

"Once on the roof the climber turns right until he reaches an iron ladder, perhaps fifteen or twenty feet high. This he ascends and, turning left, walks along the foot of the roof. This is easy, as there is the usual parapet and broadwalk. At the end of this roof we descend into a small area or sunken well. Climbing out of this (it is only about eight feet deep) we emerge on a broad, flat roof with a pinnacle at its near left-hand corner. The pinnacle is perhaps twenty five feet high and presents little difficulty. Standing on the parapet of the roof, one holds on to a gargoyle with the left hand and to a ridge above it with the right hand. Now pull up and place the left foot on another gargoyle. This is the most difficult part of an easy climb and should prove easy even to the most inexperienced, as there is only a short drop (about six feet) to the roof below. The rest is easy. The pinnacle is studded with small carvings which are perfectly sound, and one walks up them as one would up a ladder. At the top there is a good view of the lighted town, and little or no chance of the climber being seen by inquisitive eyes."

The O'Hara Pinnacle or Tottering Tower. At the moment of taking the photograph the top cross, which the climber is holding, was swaying. Note King's Chapel in the background.

The name "Tottering Tower" was given because two of the party swore that the top of the pinnacle swayed just before the photograph was taken. This climb, though fairly easy, looked extremely dangerous, because the climber had to trust small knobs about the size of a fist.

Those who look upwards by day will have noticed the two stone arches on the top of the north side. These, when one is close up to them, are surprisingly big. We said there was only one climb on the roof; these form a possible exception to our statement. They are ten or twelve feet high, and could be climbed either by the human ladder method, or by a wire-ribbon lightning conductor. At present, however, the conductor is flush with the wall, very neat and tidy, so we suggest the human ladder. Also, it is seldom wise to trust a lightning conductor near the top.

And so we will pause, to look at the view.

From here on a moonlight night one has a fine view of Cambridge. To the south King's Chapel looms mysteriously, its tapering spires stretching upwards towards the scudding clouds in unrivalled grandeur. We are level with the tops of its windows, sixty or seventy feet up, yet still it seems so gigantic that we might be looking at it from the ground. We cannot help envying those two climbers down on the roofs of Trinity Hall who once heard a neighbouring party climbing on the Chapel. What emotions would it not arouse if from here we saw two climbers near the top of those needle-like spires, small and ant-like, silhouetted minutely against the hugeness of the sky?

And then, to the north, St John's Chapel stands out menacingly across a sea of roof-tops, to send us back from excitement to a shuddering foreboding. Rumour says that it has only once been climbed, and then by a party of experts, heavily roped. Even the participants are silent on this subject, and rumour continues its tale that one of them fell off, and owed his life to the rope. Lest others should attempt the ascent of this terrible climb and perish, they swore themselves to secrecy (telling only enough people to ensure the perpetuation of their epic) and went off to try Everest instead. In vain we have tried to find out more about this climb; the echoes of the past are muffled.

The photographers have not yet attempted this building; that is why we shudder as we stand on the Old Library and look at it.

Below us the roofs of Trinity Hall strike a more cheerful note. There is nothing at all exciting about them, but it is pleasant to look down on them from such a height.

A sound of steps in Senate House Passage brings us to the edge, full of peeping curiosity. A proctor is passing below, moving until his head is in a direct line with his feet, a speck without height. Rather inconsequently, we wonder what would happen if we spat, and how far his august form would have moved from the point of impact. Would he attribute it to an owl or a bat? Or would he continue imperturbably onwards, like Queen Victoria with a couple of train-bearers? We shall never know.

The roofs of the Old Library are an infant's paradise. Everything is uneven, a jumbled confusion of slopes, leaded walks, iron ladders, and rotten planks bridging shallow gaps. The whole forms a square, built round the inner court where law students now swarm by day. It is great fun exploring all round, and one always hopes to find a store of bags labelled "gold", and stowed away by some medieval villain. And if one fails in this one may at least find, as we did once, a builder's collar and studs, forgotten in the rush to down tools. The more naughty members of the party may feel the urge to cry "boo" to the caretaker to see what action he will take, but they should be restrained. Crying "boo" at people is not consistent with good climbing.

And now it is time to go home. Eager Egbert is in lodgings, and must be in by twelve. That is why he will not always be able to come with us unless – well, it's a top-floor window, but after this he *might* be able to get up to it. Knowing Egbert, we think he will.

And so good-night. And remember, Egbert, please, *black* gym-shoes and not those white things you use for squash.

CHAPTER SEVEN

Here and There

"Stolen waters are sweet, and bread eaten in secret is pleasant"

Proverbs ix. 17

BESIDES THE Old Library, there are numbers of isolated climbs which do not fall into collegiate classification. Although the climbing is in each case very different, they all have certain common characteristics which distinguish them from college buildings. There are no petulant dons to be inadvertently awakened. No sabre-toothed porter is on his nightly prowl for blood. All is heliotrope and honeysuckle. But on the other hand, it is impossible to be away from the policeman's beat, and he may take a lot of persuading that we are not burglars should he happen to come across us. And until midnight the proctor is likely to come round the corner at any moment, very much less friendly than the policeman. Take no heed of his "Come down, sir". The bulldogs are a tough breed, but on a building they are like porkers trying to swim. Stay as high as you can. Even if you are trapped with no alternative way of descent, lie quiet. They will then think you have scrambled down the sheer face of nowhere and gone away.

On the opposite side of the river to Magdalene, on Quayside, there are two pipes running up the Officers' Training Corps. Quite a

Friend or foe? Or, alternatively, "Come down, blast you sir, come down".

Double Drain-pipe work.
The object of the climb is to sign one's name on the white board above.

worthy little climb is to go up these two pipes and pencil one's name
on the white signboard which surrounds them half-way up. We believe
that it is impossible to reach the roof by this route with the pipes in
their present state. There was nothing dramatic in the photograph
showing the policeman at the foot of the pipe; he obligingly posed
for us.

There is another pipe thirty yards to the right, on the white wall
of the corner house, of which we include a photograph. This is not to
encourage other climbers to tackle it (hardly good manners on a private
house) but because it was once the scene of a remarkable achievement.
Three climbers were on Quayside at eight o'clock one evening, prepar-

ing to drive off to one of the colleges to take some photographs. While the driver was turning the car, the second man was screwing bulbs into the reflector and the third was coiling the rope, which he threw into the car. He was without cap or gown, and when a proctor appeared thirty yards away he dived for the nearest drain-pipe (the "O'Hara Drain-pipe", see photograph). Fortunately the pipe was firmly clamped and stood away from the wall. The two overhangs presented no difficulty, and he was soon up at the top.

There were no hand- or foot-holds to help him except the pipe, and it seemed that he must come down again. Level with his head was an untrustworthy gutter, and a sloping tile roof stretched up above. While the proctor and two bulldogs stood below watching him with awe, he slowly worked his way up on to the roof and out of sight. The sloping corner by a gabled window enabled him to make the holdless ascent up an incline of forty-five degrees to the horizontal. When we asked him afterwards how he enjoyed this last little bit, he said he could remember nothing except a tremendous boom of laughter from one of his colleagues down below. Crossing over the roof, he found a possible pipe on the other side, and while the proctor was investigating inside the house he came safely down to earth.

Now comes one of those little touches whereby truth scores over fiction. Instead of walking away for five minutes, or taking a stance down the street whence he could watch with safety, he must needs wait in the hope of joining the little crowd that was gathering to watch. The idea of watching the bulldogs' teeth combing the roof-tops for a man who was standing close at hand, an interested spectator, appealed to his Irish imagination. But alas! He was never destined to join the onlookers, for he was caught. One of the bulldogs at least was disappointed at this end to a gallant attempt to evade capture, and confided

The O'Hara Drain-pipe, by Quayside, near Magdalene.
One of our party made a remarkable escape from a proctor up this pipe.

to the writer that it was "the smartest bit of work" he had ever seen. We were inclined to agree.

And now we must move on. The climbs of this chapter are dotted about Cambridge, and we may not stand and gape like the two men whom we saw an hour later on Quayside, listening to the words of a witness as he pointed at the pipe.

The easiest of these scattered climbs is the ascent of the Divinity Schools, opposite to the Main Gate of St John's. The building falls back, thus breaking up the climb into two stages. Both of these are easy.

On the front, running up by the right-hand window, is a short pipe. From the bowl of this pipe the parapet can be reached, and in five or ten seconds from leaving the ground the climber should be safely over. Keeping close to the right-hand wall, we edge past a worthy in a niche. A sloping ledge on the wall leads up to the farther wall, and we must go along this ledge. It is rather narrow, and we must go with arms stretched out sideways, close to the wall. The fact that there is a drop of only five feet behind us deprives this manoeuvre of excitement and we reach another short pipe.

From the ledge we can reach the bowl of this, which is about four feet short of the top. A wriggle and a press-up, and we can reach the top with one hand.

Should anyone find this difficult, let him turn towards St John's Street, when he will find that he can wedge the length of his left foot between the pipe and the wall. This is not necessary, but some people find it easier.

On the roof we turn right, and walk along the leads for about five yards, until we can go no farther. A somewhat rotten wooden ladder takes us up over the slates and down the other side, where we find ourselves by the Onion. This is a squat, domed tower surmounted by a stone cross.

Divinity Schools, by the Onion. The strange blur of light is the moon.

Divinity Schools, St John's Street.

With a long step we can get across on to it, and with a careful press-up we can get on to the parapet chest high. This is as high as the single climber should go. From the parapet he can easily reach the stone knobs near the top, but they are not safe – indeed, one or two are missing, dislodged presumably by previous climbers. For two climbers it should make quite a pretty little climb.

On one occasion we wanted to take a photograph of a climber on St John's Main Gate across the road. It was decided to flash from the side of the Onion, with the camera half-way towards the Hawk's Club on the ground. With a string round his waist the flash-man went up to the roof and hauled the apparatus up silently after him. With folds of loose string all around him he stumbled over the wooden ladder and took up his position by the Onion.

As the camera- and flash-men could not see each other, they had arranged to whistle when each was ready, and then the flash-man was to whistle four times and flash on the fourth. Before this, it should be said, the climber was to wave a white handkerchief four times when he was ready.

All started according to schedule. The handkerchief waved, whistle answered whistle, and four pips announced the critical moment. The camera clicked, the flash-man pressed, and the climber tried to look dramatic. But nothing happened; the apparatus had failed. The flash-man tried again with the same result.

To an outside observer the next five minutes must have been faintly ludicrous. The flash-man lost his head, and kept up a continual barrage of pips while he shook the apparatus, banged the reflector and pressed the trigger. The climber, slightly confused, flapped a handkerchief with equal vigour although no one took the slightest notice of him. So that no one should say that he was wasting time, the camera-man let off an occasional toot. Then, in the stillness which followed, the flash went off "of its own accord" as the flash-man said. It was a good twenty minutes before he had come down, recharged the apparatus and gone up again. The unfortunate climber on the top of the Main Gate nearly died of exposure; it was a chilly night with a strong wind blowing.

It took us three attempts to get photographs of the Divinity Schools. On the first occasion all went well, but the photograph failed to come out; on the second, the proximity of a plain-clothes detective marred things; on the third, we succeeded.

From the wing to the top of the central part of the building is about ten feet, connected by iron hoops fixed into the wall. Or, if you prefer it, there is a stump of drain-pipe. The upper roof is not very interesting. It is possible without further climbing to get to the top, even higher than the Onion.

The climbing of the Senate House is one of those misty legends which owe their glamour to their complete lack of definition. We have heard the ascent attributed to various people, notably to a certain athlete whose name was very widely known for his versatility and outstanding achievements. There is something more appealing about an unverified legend than the strict facts and dates of history, and we have purposely refrained from writing to ask him whether there is truth in the legend.

The easiest way to prove that a climb has been done is to repeat it. We therefore set ourselves to study the Senate House, and found it tantalizing, in that it looks easy, and yet had defied the efforts of our various friends who had tried it. A number of chimneys run up its faces, but they are either too narrow or too broad, and too shallow into the wall. We managed to struggle a few feet up one of the broad ones, and so dare not say that the chimneys are impossible.

A possible way for two climbers might be the windows on the south

The South Face of Caius.
A: The hang-over on to the Senate House; B: Awkward traverse.

*The South Face of Caius. This must be climbed
in order to reach the drop over on to the Senate House.*

face. They have ledges nearly two feet broad, and an upper window might be reached by a climber standing on his companion's shoulders. He would then lower a short cord or rope for number two to follow, and they would then have to repeat the process on the ledge of the upper window, at a height of twenty feet or more, to reach the roof. This may sound fanciful, and we only offer it as being, in our opinion, the most likely way in which the Senate House could be climbed direct.

The easiest way, which may perhaps be considered an evasion, is to climb the face of Caius and drop across the Senate House Passage, a distance of about seven feet at the narrowest part. Having decided to do this, we tackled the south face of Caius.

Climbing up the window to the right of the archway, reach the sill of the window above. Then a hand-traverse along a ledge to the left, past the pipe until the left foot can reach the curved flange, projecting for an inch from the wall, above the archway. Should you prefer it, you can walk along the ledge, using the pipe for balance until you can reach the window-sill on the left. Standing on this window-sill, your only handhold is the cross-bar, waist-high.

Standing on the steel bar of the window-sill (see photograph) and with one hand on the cross-bar, you can just reach a small ledge above your head. With both hands on this (it is only two or three inches broad) pull up on to the cross-bar. You can now reach a ledge just over two feet above the other. The lower ledge is now chest-high, and there are no foot-holds between it and the cross-bar below. The obtuse angle to the main wall formed by the base of a bay window now helps.

Laying the left forearm flat on the lower ledge to the left, and holding the upper ledge with the right hand, pull with the right hand and push up with the left. With a knee on the lower ledge it is comparatively easy to scramble up. At this stage of the climb one is acutely conscious of how much depends on the soundness of the stone of the two ledges. Fortunately, all the stone-work except the gargoyles on this building is in excellent condition.

From now on the climb is easy. With the help of a stony celebrity on the right (on whom take care to press downwards as much as possible, and not outwards and sideways) we can reach the roof-level. Over the top of the bay window, a delicate moment's traverse to the left, and we can walk along the leads to the end.

From here on to the Senate House looks pretty formidable. Tradition has it that a drunkard once jumped across, and having sobered up in splendid isolation, found that he dared not jump back. Continual coaxing and the sight of many friendly hands waiting to grab him on arrival finally caused him to cross the gulf again, and he arrived without mishap.

Our method was less dramatic. Behind the stone parapet the roof runs up very steeply, for ten or more feet. On the top is a leaded square, ten yards broad, known as the flag plateau. It is an easy scramble on to this, and three members of the party went up while the fourth tied a rope round his chest. A fifth roped himself to the outside of the stone balustrade to hold number four's feet. The flash-man and camera-man were in the street below, and the three men on the flag plateau held the rope.

The wretched man on the end of the rope found that to stand on the edge of a high building and drop forward requires will-power, and the two down below listened to his mental conflict with interest. When finally he toppled over, the rope was not paid out quick enough, and he swung round back to the wall. A second photograph was obtained of his body spanning the gap. The fact that both these photographs were spoilt by the laughable omission of the camera-man to close the shutter was an amusing detail of the evening's work.

Falling across from Caius to the Senate House.
"Some airy devil hovers in the sky." – King John, iii, 2.

On one occasion, wishing to go up on to the roof of Caius, we noticed that a first-floor window was open. The time was 12.30 a.m., and as we climbed up to it the light was turned on. It was a bedroom and the inhabitant came across to the window to draw the curtains. He told us afterwards that he saw our face leering in the darkness outside, but not the body attached to it. For a few moments his contortions and convulsions really alarmed us, but the whole affair passed off happily. His name was Stephan.*

The incident on the roof of Marks and Spencers is perhaps worth recording. It was one of the very few occasions on which any of our party trespassed on to private property, and we only record it because of the brilliant escape of one of the two men concerned.

One of the Cambridge members of our party was concerned at the lack of pinnacles in our photographs. What the lay reader wanted, he said, was not drain-pipes and chimneys, but bodies crawling over pinnacles like bumble-bees on a foxglove. There was one particular pinnacle he had in mind; the spire above Lloyds Bank at the bottom of Petty Cury.

We knew the place. The idea of climbing it had long ago occurred to us, and after prolonged study we had decided that the face of the building below the pinnacle could be climbed. We had never entertained it seriously because it was a private building, but now the pinnaclomania that was infecting the party paralysed our better judgement. We went

---

* A certain famous athlete once came to grief while climbing down from one of these first floor windows of Caius. A popular host as well as a triple blue, he annoyed the authorities by entertaining guests from other colleges after midnight, and he was anxious to avoid further trouble. One night at 12.30, during a hilarious party, he was told that the porters were about to raid his room. He hastily put all the beer glasses he could find on a tray, which he placed on one hand, and tried to climb down to the street. Even a trained waiter would have found this difficult, and in his subsequent fall he broke his ankle.

off with him to investigate.

It was a bump-supper night, and everyone in Jesus College who was not drunk appeared to be dancing round a bonfire. Our intention to investigate the Lantern (another pinnacle) in the college was frustrated by a porter, who would not allow us to go into the court in question. So we went off to look at the Lloyds pinnacle, intending to collect the rest of the party later for a photograph if the climb proved possible.

Climbing over some railings by the Central Cinema, we went from roof to roof under the brilliant glare of a full moon. Passing over Marks and Spencers we were particularly noisy, and after going up a short pipe on to a sloping roof (with the help of a chimney-stack) we came to the base of the spire.

To climb half-way up was comparatively easy, and the rest of the way was up a lightning-conductor, with no outside holds. After testing the staples, which were beautifully firm, we decided that the top might be reached. But it was a climb which should not be done more than once, as each attempt would tend to weaken the conductor, and near the top the climber's safety would hang, at the most, from two or three staples. So we returned to find the rest of the party, whom we had arranged to meet at eleven o'clock.

On the roof of the bank we heard some noises which caused us to think, but not to worry.

Having returned to the roof of Marks and Spencers, we decided to investigate the roof of the Central Cinema. But we found it necessitated a long circuit, and after sheltering for ten minutes from a shower of rain, decided to go down again. There was a ladder on to a lower roof, and the first climber was half-way down when two torches appeared on the lower roof.

Expecting to speak a few kind words to a couple of decrepit old men and then beat a hasty retreat, he went on down the ladder. He then most unexpectedly found himself in the custody of plain-clothes policemen. He was detained in a small room while they went up to look for number two. He was informed that the building was surrounded on all sides by police. While waiting, he persuaded his guard to copy down the two notices which formed the only decorations on the walls. They ran as follows:

OPTIMISM

Remember the steam kettle,

Though up to its neck in hot water,

It still continues to sing.

This was cheering; and the other:

TRY IT

Somebody said that it couldn't be done,

But he with a chuckle replied,

That maybe it couldn't,

But he was one who wouldn't say so

Until he had tried.

The upper roof was about half the size of a tennis-court, and with sheer walls on all sides they were convinced that number two could not have got away. However, there was nowhere he could hide, and he was not there, so they finally came away. Number one was led away in handcuffs, and continues in the log-book: "At the station I met several old friends, including P.C. ———, and thereafter tension relaxed". Several of them quoted various times and places where they had seen him (one Welsh sergeant quoted half a dozen), and they explained to the inspector that he was just a harmless eccentric who liked to wave to members of the Force from college roof-tops. Never was any man more thankful to have cultivated the friendship of policemen. The inspector told him not to climb in Cambridge again, and at the moment of writing, three months after the event, it remains the last climb of any of the party. The log-book records a few further, if inconsequent details:

"At 2 a.m. I left amidst the general blessings of the police force. I was anxious about C., as the Welsh sergeant had said there were pools of blood in C.'s track, and that he must be suffering from serious loss of blood. However, on the off-chance that he was pulling my leg I had professed to be hugely amused about it, and said I did not care whether C. was hurt or not. It subsequently turned out that the Welshman had been pulling my leg; he was a good man.

"As I passed M. and Spencers I saw a car outside. The manager had just turned up, three hours late. Resisting a temptation to say 'Wot, burglars? Let's catch 'em', I looked in and gently explained that I was the culprit, and had done it for fun. (This reluctance to let well alone will be my undoing some day.) The manager seemed pained and spoke reproachfully. 'Fun? My first night's sleep for a month is spoiled, and you call it fun.' I moved on.

"The car had been moved into a garage, and the place was shut up. I went to the house of an employee three hundred yards away to get a key. He sent me to Mr H., in Haig Road, Chesterton. A Robert lent me his bike, asking me first how we had done the 'Save Ethiopia' stunt* when he was on the beat. (How he knew it was us, I don't know.) 'You must have watched every step I took,' he said. 'Do you remember I spoke to a lorry driver who was standing against the wheel of his lorry?' For an incident over nine months old this is not a bad memory.

---

* To be explained in a later chapter.

'Of course we were watching', I replied, remembering neither Bobbie nor lorry. He seemed to think we had timed it very smartly, and from what he told me we must have escaped being caught by only a few minutes.

"Mr H. had once sold me a dud car for £60, but I was sorry to pull him out of bed. He came willingly and politely, but seemed a bit pained that I had not awakened more underlings first.

"I was home by 5.0."

Meanwhile number two had had an interesting escape. Without realizing what was happening, he decided that the career of a Trinity man caught on Marks and Spencers was likely to be cut short. He decided that this, if ever, was the time for blind heroism, and with a man coming up the ladder he popped up on to a smaller roof six feet higher, and raced to the east side.

Here there was a drop of twelve feet on to a small area of roof, about ten yards square. A chimney-stack enabled him to slither down, but he knew he could not get up again. On three sides there was a wall rising up; on the fourth, a drop down. If he could not find a suitable pipe in that ten yards of frontage, he must be caught, or jump.

Fortune was with him. After descending a pipe for twenty feet he did a hand-traverse across two window-ledges and came to the passage. The diagram may help the reader to understand the climber's narrative, from which we quote:

"Then out to street and looked over wall and saw it was hopeless. So back through door which I had luckily left open, and locked it on inside in case they had seen me. Then rushed into some lodgings and slap into screaming girls' bedroom. Apologized and told them to keep quiet and shot out again almost into the beam of the detectives' torches. Decided this was hopeless, so went into lodgings again

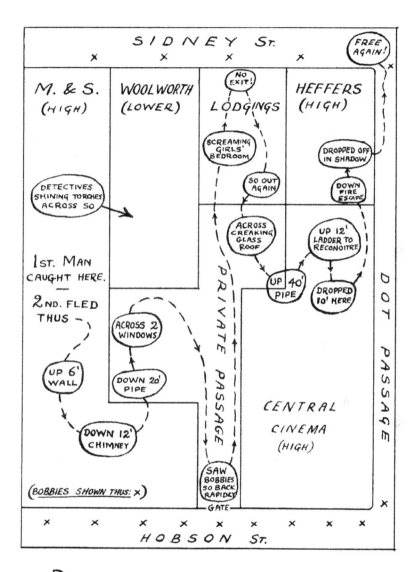

DIAGRAM OF THE ESCAPE FROM
MARKS & SPENCERS.

up a flight of stairs into an empty room overlooking Sydney Street. Thought of dropping out* as not many people about, but unfortunately an inspector was wandering about; also the drop was really excessive. So out again and saw that the guys with the torches had gone, so got across glass roof and then up about 40-ft pipe, which was tiring because absolutely smooth walls… sort of glazed bricks. At the top it seemed colossally public. I felt as though the whole town was looking until I saw everything going on quite normally below. There was a drop of 10 ft. straight ahead on to roof of cinema, but I thought if I went down I could never get up again and there seemed to be no way off, so I went aloft higher by a ladder and walked over to where I saw the stairs below (fire escape); soon beat it down there and dropped off into passage, and walked away, which was rather an anti-climax … I felt like a chase then!"

We apologize for the length of this anecdote, and now we must return to the serious climber.

The Fountain in the Market Place would be an ideal little climb but for its unsound condition. Unlike buildings belonging to the colleges, the stone is really rotten and crumbly. Even the four central arches creak beneath one's weight and feel that they might collapse at any moment, so we did not attempt to reach the top. However, it cannot stay long in its present state, for it is already half a ruin. On the off-chance that it may some day be repaired we include it in this book. It has several times been climbed in the past.

The boss in the centre of the Fountain may be used to help the climber to get into a sitting position on the arch. From there it is possible to get a hand round the corner, and if the masonry were safe the

---

* Just as well he didn't, as there were at least three bobbies watching the building on that side.

Fountain in the Market Place.

rest would be easy. At first sight it looks deceptively difficult.

As there is nearly always a policeman in the Market Place, an attempt must be carefully timed. On one occasion two of the photographers had just come down from posing for a photograph when a policeman came round the corner. The Inefficient Photographer was driving, and as the climbers wanted to stay by the Fountain they signed to him to drive on, while they kept the Fountain between themselves and the policeman.

Hopeless Harry drove round the Market Place. He then slowed up, totally unable to think what to do next, and finally went round a second time. Regardless of the fact that his behaviour was highly eccentric, considering the time and place (it was 3 a.m.), he started off on a third circuit.

The situation was ludicrous. The Robert leant his bicycle against the Guild Hall, and turned to watch the weasel-like antics of this strange vehicle. The climbers behind the Fountain, like the Foreign Minister on equally absurd but more solemn occasions, decided it was time to intervene. They shuffled off, and amiably explained the whole thing to the policeman. He was a man with a grievance against the world – he should have been a schoolmaster but for the war – but he liked the Young Idea, so all was well.

Meanwhile the Inefficient Photographer, convinced that his associates were in trouble, roared and rattled round the Market Place with more determination than ever. In his gear-changing there was something of the gabbling of a hen-turkey whose brood is threatened by a fox. The fierce rending of cog against cog must have awakened every sleeper for hundreds of yards. Finally the policeman asked to see his licence, and all enjoyed a laugh together, Hopeless Harry the loudest of all. It is little incidents such as this that make night climbing worth while.

After this it would be well to leave the Market Place. Proceeding down Corn Exchange Street, the Drain-pipe specialist is tempted by a number of stark-looking pipes on the right. The Chimney specialist hastily drags him on, and we abut into the east end of Pembroke Street.

From here down to the Trumpington Road is the happy hunting-ground of all advanced parties. A Guide-book of the size of the *Guide to Trinity* could be written round this fertile three hundred yards of road. We have spent hours lounging along here, tracing possible climbs over the face of the buildings, memorizing, whether we would or not, almost every ledge and hand-hold for hundreds of yards. For the moment we will confine ourselves to two drain-pipes.

At the corner of Corn Exchange Street is a thin lead drain-pipe running up past two windows to the roof. We decided to try this one.

The pipe runs close to the wall, is slightly loose and not at all strong. The stone is slotted, but the slots are so narrow that it is only possible to get one finger behind the pipe. If the slots were wider and deeper it would be possible to walk up as though up a ladder, but as it is the climb is difficult. The photographers got no farther than the ledge of the upper window; they only attempted it once.

On this ledge the climber concerned found himself in a predicament. It was a bitter night, freezing hard and with a biting east wind. The heavy strain on his fingers had quite numbed them, so that he could not get up or down. Fortunately on this window-ledge there are two ornamental pillars, round one of which he was able to pass the knotted rope, and so descend. It is a nasty climb.

Ten yards to the left there is another drain-pipe which is much more attractive. It is of iron, firm, thick, and stands well away from the wall. To get to it a six-foot wall must be crossed. Hanging down at arm's length on the other side, one expects a drop of a few inches.

Drain-pipe in Downing Street.

Prudently looking down before releasing one's hold on the wall, one is horrified to see the ground fifteen or twenty feet below the top of the wall. However, there is a light iron bridge a few yards away, and one can get across on to this.

From this bridge one must get on to a window-ledge, six or seven feet above. This is not easy, but one is helped by a short length of pipe which sticks out four inches from the wall and makes a good foot-hold. With a traverse of a few feet to the right, we get on to the drain-pipe. Although we have only climbed six or seven feet, it is comforting to know there is a drop of twenty feet below us.

The first time a member of the party climbed this pipe, he found it extremely tiring, and announced when a few feet from the top that he could go no farther. He was wearing gym-shoes, and found it very hard to get a good grip with them. To encourage him the flashlight failed, and he had to come down again. He refused to go up a second time until later in the evening.

This time he found it much easier. Instead of trying to edge his feet sideways into the slots, he kept his toes to the wall, with the heels pointing outwards. Like this he was able to walk straight up the pipe without strain or effort, and when he came down again was scarcely out of breath. This climber has developed a peculiar habit of saying "Goodie, goodie" at the end of every climb.

Every quarter of an hour or so some machine in this building makes a peculiar noise, rising from a low buzz to a loud whine, and then down again. Whether or not it is a burglar-alarm we cannot say, but if it is, then it is as ineffectual against roof-climbers as a scarecrow to a pair of magpies.

Leaving this pipe at last, we go down the street towards Trumpington Road. Besides the innumerable severe climbs on the right, there are several on the left, on the north face of Pembroke and on Pembroke Bridge. At the bottom we turn left, and proceed for a few hundred yards.

And so we come to the Fitzwilliam Museum. At the time, our party of photographers had dwindled to two members, who were staying over fifty miles from Cambridge. It was between Christmas and the New Year, that unwanted corner of time which has wedged itself unobtrusively into the depths of fog and ice, forgotten from year to year. We had been sleeping heavily by day and going off again in the evening. Let the log-book speak:

"Rising about twelve, we went to collect the photos. Of the sixteen we had taken, sixteen came out. This was very satisfactory; some were quite good, some out of focus.

"After supper, we still had not a third man. I called on Jack S., but found him out. Jim B. was also unable to come. At 10.30 I was telephoning to Mrs. G. in Cambridge, and found to my joy that Ronnie was staying with her. So we arranged to pick him up at midnight, and left just after 10.40 p.m. We had previously spent a sociable evening at the club, and so were not feeling much like climbing. However, I could not waste Eric on his last night.

"It was just on midnight when we picked up Ronnie. Parking the car in Fitzwilliam St., we slipped over the wall into the grounds of the museum, and round to the Lion Chimney on the right. It had turned much colder, and the others shivered as I ran back to fetch a spare bulb and the torch.

"They took a photo of me at the top of the chimney (the same as the other night, only with the camera farther away and in front). This chimney, above one of the lions at the north-east corner, is of an ideal width, with vertical grooves to keep the feet (and body) from slipping sideways.

The Fitzwilliam Museum. Lion Chimney.

The Fitzwilliam Museum. Lion Chimney.

"Then down again, and round to the back. On the way we noted the chimney at the north-west corner was also an easy one.

"The chimney at the back is half-way along the west wall. The building drops back about ten feet, at the point where the high side building is joined by the lower middle building. To reach this point one had to crunch along some very noisy gravel, and some buildings beyond appeared to be occupied. A large bush of bamboo or similar growth screens the bottom of the chimney.

"Surmounting a broad ledge at chest-level, one stands comfortably in the chimney. With one's back in the corner, the opposite wall stretches two and a half feet to the left. Owing to the deep vertical grooves, one can chimney against the outer corner, which makes it easy. The left hand can get a good grip on the corner, where a narrow neck of stone provides a rounded hold which fits the palm of the hand.

"To complete the luxury, there is a wire-rope lightning-conductor in the corner on the right. It is rusted, and if one uses it one must climb with one's eyes shut. Eric did not notice it until near the top, and managed quite well without it.

"The only part needing special care is the ledge eight feet from the top. This narrows the chimney for a distance of two feet and with care can easily be surmounted without the conductor. We got a photo of this chimney. Eric was not long in joining me on the roof. Ronnie was impressed by our silhouettes on the roof against the moonlight.

"From the roof to the top of the building on the left was a good twenty feet up a vertical wall. Further, there was a ledge half-way up projecting for four feet.

"A strip conductor makes the climb possible. Holding it in one hand, one reaches back at an acute angle and grasps the ledge, on to which one pulls one's self. From there to the top is quite easy, and we sat on the

The Fitzwilliam Chimney at the back.

top wall for a couple of minutes studying the geography of the place.

"Immediately in front of us was a dome, rising for fifteen feet from a roof seven feet below us.

"Eric was about to drop on to this roof when I saw the reflections on it in the moonlight. It appeared to be of glass. Eric agreed that it looked like glass, but wondered by what architectural device a massive stone dome could be supported in the middle of it. This was certainly strange.

"The stone of the dome was interspersed with narrow windows, below each of which there was a ledge just above roof-level. On to one of these ledges I gingerly lowered myself.

"A hollow ping and the feel under my foot aroused my suspicions. The suspicion that one feels at the circus when the strong man juggles with gigantic spheres of steel came to my mind, and I stooped down. Nor was I wrong. The stone was simply sheet metal painted grey, as the drumming of my fingers conveyed to Eric. It was not long before I was back on the wall.

"The colossal impudence of putting a dummy dome on a roof left us with a great respect for the architect. What manner of man was this, who with a few sheets of tin and a pot of paint could conceive the idea of imitating the stately curves of Constantinople? It was stupendous.

"More than stupendous, it might become revolutionary. What had been done once might be done again, on a very much wider scale. With a pot of paint and a few sheets of corrugated iron, we might have feudal castles dotted once more over the land, as realistic to their inhabitants as to the stream of American sightseers they would attract. And provided William the Bad did not come with Ye Ancient Battering Rams, or the wind did not blow too hard, rural England would be the richer for their added beauty. Of course, if a swarm of bees got between the inner and the outer wall, yokels for fifty miles around would think that the tocsin was sounding for a new crusade, but this would not matter.

"And yet it is slightly sad to think that even a building could wish to seem different from what it was. This was the first time we had caught a building using cosmetics, and we were abashed. Without more ado we returned to the lower roof.

"A policeman testing doors on the opposite side of the street now attracted our attention. He tested the gate of Fitz Billy and then, to our horror, walked in.

"I shouted down to warn Ronnie. He was taking a stroll thirty yards away, and rushed back with mighty crunchings to hide the paraphernalia (and himself) in the bush. The Robert heard nothing, and his measured tread walked by and faded away. P.C. X later in the night was vastly amused by this anecdote. He kept chuckling to himself, and told us it was P.C. YZ, and that he had to go round the Fitz Billy six times in the night, at intervals of an hour and a quarter. 'He's only just married, so you wouldn't expect him to hear you.' We gave P.C. X the photograph of himself at the foot of the C.U.O.T.C. drain-pipe, with Eric half-way up.

"After that to St John's. After priming Ronnie how to work the camera…"

But the rest of the activities of the photographers that night does not fall into this chapter. Suffice it to say that Ronnie was not primed enough; he bungled the photograph.

CHAPTER EIGHT

St John's

"Hark, hark! I hear
The strain of strutting Chanticleer
Cry Cock-a-doodle-doo"

Tempest, I. 2

"The Devil damn thee black, thou cream-faced loon"

Macbeth

AND NOW we will go to St John's. By now our novice of the first few chapters is becoming more self-confident, and occasionally starts off up a climb without permission. In the caution of our staid experience we find ourselves being left behind, and must see to it. Have we gone stale? Here was a fellow who still considers himself a novice, leading up climbs where we hesitate to follow. It is all very well to say, "By Jove, that was a good climb; I wouldn't have done it myself"; if we say it too often, he will believe us. He is as eager to earn a reputation as we are to justify our own. "I will not yield, to kiss the ground before young Malcolm's feet – lay on, Macduff, and damned be he that first cries, Hold, enough!" In other words, we must all tackle severe climb after climb and pretend to enjoy it.

St John's from St John's Street.
First pitch of Main Gate climb. There are two pitches to follow.

St John's Main Gate. The second pitch.

Here we are outside the Main Gate. As we stand facing it there are three drain-pipes on the wall dropping away to the left. Of these we choose the middle one, because it fulfils all the requirements. It is reasonably firm, it stands away from the wall, and there is a zigzag half-way up which makes it easier than its two rivals. All these pipes are of lead.

The first part of this pipe is the most difficult. From the kink in the pipe one can step on to a window-sill, and thence with a short pull-up on to the arched tops of the windows on each side. We believe the window on the right to be occupied by a porter or a resident don, but there is little need to disturb him. The pipe does not rattle.

St John's Main Gate. Third and last pitch.

After surmounting the battlements and taking a well-earned rest, we turn to the right. Here we mount a gabled window, and step from gable to gable until we reach the last one by the square tower. We now come to our second drain-pipe.

Within arm's reach from the top of the gable the pipe recedes over a sloping ledge. From here upwards it stands out from the wall, and it is an easy scramble on to the ledge.

From the sloping ledge it is but a short distance to the horizontal ledge on the left, a few feet short of the top. This is an awkward moment. The pipe stops level with this ledge, and the question is how to get up the last few feet. It is impossible to reach straight up. To the left is a gap, but it appears to be out of reach. By moving the feet along the ledge, however, it is possible to reach this gap, and in a moment the climber is on top of the tower.

The last fifteen feet, up any of the corner turrets, is made easy by a short drain-pipe on each. Above the bowl of the pipe there is a square

Main Gate of St John's up to the statue.

aperture through the wall, to allow the rain-water to pass through. This provides the last hand-hold, and the top is reached.

This climb was unique among the wanderings of the photographers, in that they did it "on the spur of the moment". At the time they were on their way into Trinity, to do the Fourth Court climb. The restless Eric started testing the pipes to the left of the Main Gate, and before the rest knew where they were he was near the top, shouting for a photograph. He was kept waiting for a couple of minutes, in the position where he is shown in the photograph, and then went up to the battlements.

A much more difficult climb is the ascent to the first window, above the Main Gate. The climber must start with the help of a friendly shoulder, and from then on keep close to the left-hand wall. A small stone pillar runs up about nine inches from the wall, on the outside of the ornamentations. The climber must keep by this pillar, and can wedge his foot between it and the wall; it is a severe test for the arms.

From the window-ledge a climber in playful mood may leave his gown or surplice on the statue in the middle. This would probably cause considerable surprise to the authorities.

A much more genteel climb is getting on to the Ivy Arch, fifty yards to the south of the Main Gate. The name dates back to the days when it was covered in ivy; since then it has had a shave, and is now quite spruce-looking. Architecturally, it is rather unimaginative. Built to conceal the fact that behind the gate it adorns is a vulgar back-yard, it goes up in broad steps to a veritable plateau on the top.

We climb on to the arch by mounting the railings at the left-hand side.* A stone knob at the foot of the curved flange above the gate provides a foot-hold, and we get on to the bottom step of the arch.

---

* These have since been removed.

Above the Ivy Arch.
Trinity Chapel on the left. Note the flash-man in front.

On this ledge we once left a camera, and only remembered it when we were twenty miles from Cambridge.

From the top of the arch on to the roof requires a moment's care, and the roof-hiker is now free to tramp round the first three courts of the college, and peer down on the Bridge of Sighs. Or he may go up the steep slope of the roof close by the arch. The raised stone coping provides an edge on which he can grip.

A climb which looks easy, but is really quite severe, is the west face of the Third Court. There is an archway leading through on to the Bridge of Sighs, and over this there is a succession of ledges, going up to the roof. The difficulty is that there is not much additional help to get up on to each ledge, and it is a matter of awkward press-ups, each one a few feet higher from the ground, and by that much the more unpleasant. The route up is fairly obvious, but this does not make it any easier. Coming down is quite a simple business.

And now we will go round to the back gate, on the west side of the river, and climb over the railings at the side. (This, for some reason, is one of the things which the more clumsy members of the party always find difficulty in doing. It is perfectly simple and straightforward.) We then move along towards the college buildings, one or two members of the party being sure to trip over the wire at the side of the grass.

Coming to the outside of New Court, we find a gateway on the south side known as the Eagle Gateway. A pair of buttresses on each side offer a little chimneying practice. This is a good place to bring a novice to teach him to chimney, because of its complete isolation. It is quite easy to get on to the roof of the cloisters by either of these chimneys, and for those who like drain-pipes there is a splendid one at the east end, three feet from the cloisters inside the court. It stands away from the wall and the iron bindings, besides being in pairs, are

By the Eagle Gateway. On to the roof of the cloisters.

Start of the traverse of the Bridge of Sighs. One of the hardest climbs in Cambridge.

broad and flat. We have not been up this, but from the roof of the cloisters it would not be very difficult. One of the party came down it on a rope, and reported that it was dead easy.

And so we come to the Bridge of Sighs.

The complete traverse of the bridge was first done, we believe, in 1923 or 1924. It involves some of the prettiest balancing problems in Cambridge, with a ducking as the only penalty for a clumsy climber. The beauty of it is that once the climber has got on to the bridge, on the west side, he cannot get back again. Willy-nilly, he must complete what he has begun.

The climb starts from the lawn close to the south-west corner of the bridge. A broad stone wall, two feet high, bounds the lawn from the water ten feet below. From this wall one steps across on to the ledge of a buttress which projects obliquely from the corner. The buttress is about two feet wide and four feet long, and the lack of hand-holds is countered by the fact that the flat palms can grip against the wall as one goes round the two corners. As one comes round the second corner, one is face to face with the hardest part of the climb.

Moving as far along the ledge of the buttress as possible while hold-ing the corner with the left hand, one can reach nearly to the end of the buttress. From here to the main wall there is a gap of about four feet, with nothing but an expanse of wall on the other side. This gap must be crossed.

The fact that the climber is facing the wrong way makes it more difficult for him. Releasing his hold with his left hand, he must swing round as he falls and move his feet round on the ledge. Once he has fallen across, he must work along to the right, where a buttress projects from the bridge. By now the worst is over. Moving the feet down about fifteen inches on to a second ledge, one can step across on to a pointed

Third Court, St John's. A difficult and exposed climb. When the third climber was above the archway to the left of the lower climber, six dons passed underneath.

ornamentation on the second buttress. A little further balancing, and one is on the bridge itself.

At the far side a sort of ornamental pillar on the bridge enables one to mount on to the top, where two alternatives present themselves. One is to climb up on to the roof of Third Court; this looks as though it might be the easier way, though we know no one who has tried it. The other alternative is to climb down in the north-east corner. This involves making use of the stone-work to the left of the pipe (looking down) until one can grasp the bowl and so descend.

Once off the bridge, one must move along the side of the river for twenty yards and then round to the right, past what the *Roof-Climber's Guide to St John's* calls the "Furnace Hole". A pretty climb for about fifteen feet brings us down into the Third Court.

In our opinion, the whole traverse of the Bridge of Sighs is extremely severe from a technical point of view, without the usual grimness of a severe climb. It is described in the *Cambridge Review* of 1924. Onlookers seem to find it especially entertaining, and their care-free laughter seems to continue the harmony of splashing waters which is the last thing one hears before going under. If we could remember what Wordsworth had to say on the subject we would quote him.

> Five lawyers ate a cow,
>
> And if you wonder how,
>
> We agree,
>
> You and me,
>
> They couldn't do it now —

which, as you will agree, has nothing to do with it.

The most fitting climb to end a chapter on St John's is the ascent of the New Tower, above the New Court. Compared with most of the climbs in St John's it is easy, but nevertheless the height makes it thrilling.

Pipe inside New Court. The lower roof is that of the cloisters.

It falls into stages; the fifty feet from the ground to the roof, and the forty feet up the tower. The second half is considerably the harder.

To reach the roof we go up the Drain-pipe Chimney, halfway along the outer west wall. Two drain-pipes run from the ground to the battlements in the lee of a buttress set at an angle to the main wall. The right-hand pipe is loose in two places, and should not be trusted too far.

Up as far as the top of the bay window on the right is really very easy. The pipe runs up past four windows on the left, at the top and bottom of which a stone foot-hold can be found. The climber may go up as though up an exposed pipe (with the comfort of the buttress behind) or he can chimney between the buttress and the pipe. In the dark the climber goes on quite happily until he realizes with a shock that the buttress has tapered away, and he is almost on top of the bay window.

(A word of warning, incidentally, about this window top. Coming down from the roof, one expects it to be flat, whereas actually it is sloping. This produces for a moment a nasty sensation of diving outwards.)

From the top of the bay window the last twelve feet must be climbed on the exposed pipe. Do not touch the right-hand pipe here. Use the one on the left, and the top of the window as a foot-hold. It is narrow and sloping, but as the leg is pressing inwards, it is as good as a flat ledge.

The pipe ends three feet short of the battlements. There is no bowl; it just stops dead. The last few inches pass through a ledge, and so one can grasp the top with confidence. A stretch on to the battlement, and one is safely on the roof.

The log-book will now be allowed to speak without comment:

"At about 9.00 p.m. we parked the car in the lane opposite the back gate of St John's. A couple of dons taking the evening air frightened us, and sent us off when we had just got the things out of the car. Stopping at Quayside we walked to Trinity.

97

Drain-pipe chimney. The last man.

"As we entered, a porter about to go to Nevile's Court waited for us, jangled his keys and followed ten yards behind. In gym shoes and polo sweaters, and with all our impedimenta, we must have looked a villainous trio. We talked loudly of butterflies.

"Feeling suspect, we called on M., where Willy and I each smoked an excellent cigar, and we all had a glass of beer. Then away, out of Trinity.

"At the Blue Boar I collected a blue skirt which Dorothy G. had lent me.* In West Road Willy took off his trousers and buttoned it with difficulty round his waist. Making his scarf into a sort of hat, he flaunted the Fitzwilliam colours on the face of Newnham. A pair of gloves was inside his pullover, and most of his right leg showed in a crack at the side of the skirt.

"Then to St John's, to the Drain-pipe Chimney. With the rope round my waist I reached the battlements without difficulty, followed in the order Willy, impedimenta, John. Both got up without using the rope, and the impedimenta were got up without clanking. From the top Willy took a photo of John while I flashed.

"Before starting the evening Willy and I had both decided we had flu, and had nearly called the evening off. Up here there was a strongish wind, and I at least was cold and prickly the whole time. Willy looked considerably worse, and very watery-eyed. While we were climbing it was all right, but there was a lot of standing about, and several times I

---

* The acquisition of this skirt recalls a pretty tale. We were talking in the Market Place to a prominent member of the C.U.B.C., a man of short stature but gigantic girth, when the said Dorothy came into sight. She did not know our companion, but politely stopped to pass the time of day. Hereupon inspiration seized us. We cried "Dorothy, can this man borrow your skirt?" and when the answer was a profuse blush we thought the abruptness of our question was the cause. However, the real cause transpired later. By a paltry eighteen inches the skirt failed to girdle the strong man's waist, and someone else had to pose for the photograph.

Newnham, or "Girls will be Girls".

felt quite dizzy, as earlier in the evening.

"Following the leads round, one has to step from one battlement to the next at the corner. Rather unexpectedly after a quiet walk round one finds one's self looking down for fifty feet straight below. Then along by New Court, up some slates, on to a ledge and over some more battlements and one is at the foot of the tower.

"We chose the face down which comes the lightning conductor.

"The old conductor, a rusty wire-rope thing up which D. went for the first six feet, has been replaced by a formidable new affair. Of the ribbon type, it is about four times as massive as any I have ever seen, and clamped close to the wall. I tried in vain to pull it away.

"The two buttresses on either side appear to offer the possibility of chimneying. However, they diverge too much and one slips. From a man's shoulders one can stand with a foot on each, because they slope away from the vertical. One can now reach a ledge to the front and above one's head. A scramble lands one on a sort of terrace, a yard wide and two yards long.

"If the climber be alone, he can manage this first part by taking one of the neighbouring faces, where a clockless circle of stone provides the necessary holds.* Thus for the first twelve feet.

"The next twelve feet are the most difficult part of the climb.

"There are windows on each face of the Tower. The Tower becomes a couple of yards narrower in diameter at the foot of these windows.

---

* A climber now in the Antarctic once saw in these blind clock-faces the means of a clever practical joke. One night he painted four dials in the place obviously meant to receive them, and the next day the Master sent for the Head Porter to tell him that the clock on New Tower had stopped. The porter promised to see to it, and sent a man up to see whether it merely wanted winding up, or needed repairing. This man was the first to realize that there was no clock on New Tower. Legend says that the perpetrator of this joke, disguised as a travelling watch-maker, offered to mend the clock for five shillings, and then painted the hands in a different position. He tells us that this legend is untrue, much as we would like to believe it.

New Tower, St John's.

Pillars rear up at the outside corners and are joined to the Tower by an arch of sloping stone, festooned on the upper side with ornamentations that should not be trusted too far. The difficulty is to get up the length of this pillar.

"At arm's length above, wedge-shaped tongues of stone pointing downwards give some help, but not a complete hold. D. recalls that he used back-and-knee methods, and the *Guide to St John's* refers to this as an alternative way. The Guide prefers the method of getting on to the outside of the pillar and swarming up. Personally I used what I consider to be an easier way than either of these.

"The window was divided down the middle by a vertical bar of stone. From here to the pillar is just too broad for chimneying. Place a foot as high as possible on this bar. Then, making as much use as possible of the semi-hold above, place a foot on the pillar behind and straddle the gap. Although too broad for chimneying, it allows of this, and you can get a hold on the arch. From now on it is merely a wriggle to get on to the arch, and the rest of the way is practically a stone ladder to the pinnacle. Willy got two photographs.

"As we were moving back the clock struck twelve, and a porter moved about New Court, turning out the lights. Willy and I crouched behind battlements while John moved boldly along, visible in the lamp-light or silhouetted against the sky. Nothing came of his intrepidity, although he sounded very loud to us as we crouched and listened.

"Coming down, the temptation is to take the left pipe, as it is more nearly over the bay window. Both Willy and John started with this error. Take the right (looking down) and you can use the top of the window as a foot-hold.

"We took over two hours over this climb, and did no more."

There is little to add, except that the three photographs taken were

Daylight ascent of the New Tower.

not good enough, and that six repetitions of the climb were needed to produce satisfactory results. On one occasion it was so dark in the chimney that the writer was unable to see his hand when he held it up in front of his eyes. On another occasion, in the early light of dawn, we saw a porter in Trinity standing by the river, looking at us. Hence the quotations at the beginning of this chapter. A rapid ascent of the Tower was made for a daylight photograph and by an extremely rapid descent we were away in time. This was soon after two men had been rusticated for climbing King's Chapel, and the ascent of the last forty feet after he had been seen, with the prospect of a ninety foot descent before he could get away, was a good performance. The climber was in his last term, and desperately anxious not to be sent down, but he completed the job. On yet another occasion, in one of the deep rectangular cavities which occur periodically in the "bicycle track" to drain off the rain-water, we found a murdered swan. Stuffed away in the hole in the roof above the Bridge of Sighs with its neck lying along its back, it had been laid as far as possible from human gaze. The next time we visited the roof it had gone. Who had killed it, and why he had gone to so much trouble to conceal it, is a question that may never be answered. But since a climber would hardly be likely to climb up to the roof and haul up a dead swan for fifty feet after him, the finger of accusation points at the dons or porters. It reminds us of the old Limerick, known to most of the undergraduates of Cambridge:

There was a young man of St John's
Who tried to shoot one of the swans:
The voice of the porter
Cried, "Come out of the water,
Those swans are reserved for the dons".

Thus was a prophecy fulfilled in a most surprising manner.

St John's Back Gate.

CHAPTER NINE

St John's Chapel

IT IS with some hesitation that we write this chapter, as being of a climb we have neither done nor attempted. For a long time it was at the back of our minds and we came close to the attempt, so that on one or two nights we debated whether to visit the tower of this building or go elsewhere. Then, as one or another of our best climbers had to leave us, it was shelved away and forgotten. There seems to be a conspiracy of silence among all who are supposed to have climbed it, and we have had little response from the half-dozen people whom we have interrogated.

Nevertheless, from our investigations we were convinced that the climb was possible, and therefore had probably been done. This made the silence all the more baffling. One of those whom we suspected of having been in the party that first climbed it told us that one of the party fell off, and only the skilful belaying of the rope had saved a serious accident. Rightly or wrongly, we decided that this was the cause of the silence.

Two of the best climbers of their respective generations told us that they considered the climb impossible. In each case they found it comparatively easy to reach the top of the windows, fifteen or twenty feet

St John's Chapel.

below the top of the tower, but found the overhang which confronted them to be insurmountable. On the other hand, a friend quoted so eminent an authority as the writer of the first edition of the *Guide to Trinity* as saying that the climb was not unduly difficult, and had been done several times, roped and unroped. So we decided to see for ourselves.

The writer obtained written leave from the dean to go up the spiral staircase in the tower "to look at the view". He took a camera and photographed the climb from above, which was not on the whole very helpful. However, the difficulty can be seen in the photograph taken from the ground.

Where the windows on the tower begin to arch over, there is a ledge on the pillars between them. To shift on to this ledge, and then lean back over the top of the window when there is a dearth of hand-holds above, may at first sight appear to be impossible. If it is to be done, the climber must get as high as he can in the window and use the small round window in the apex as a hand-hold. Then, with the other hand, he must get a grip on one of the small ornamental pillars which run from between the windows up to the top.

From the ground, these pillars appear flush with the wall and utterly useless to a climber. It is impossible to see, as one can from the roof, that they are square, with only one edge touching the wall. With the hands and forearms on the incut faces, and his knees gripping on the pointed edges, a man should be able to swarm up fairly easily. The exposure would make it unpleasant, but once he had got from the window to the pillar the climb should be straightforward. Near the top of each pillar is a small gap between the pillar and the wall which should provide an excellent finger-grip.

Besides getting on to the pillar, it struck us that there would be one further difficulty, which does not appear from the ground. This is getting from the pillar, which stops about a yard below the top, through the balustrade. It may not be so bad as it seems, but from the top it looks nasty.

From the ground to the roof of the Chapel is within the scope of a moderate climber. Several of our party have done it, and by two different routes. The more usual way is to take a drain-pipe by one of the buttresses, and make as much use as possible of the saint on the buttress and the arrow-point canopy above his head.

About fifteen years ago two climbers were on the roof of this building, with the intention of assaulting the tower. It was a winter's evening, and as they struggled up the steep roof up to the ridge they dislodged a number of tiles with an alarming amount of noise. A small crowd gathered by the lamplight in Bridge Street to watch. The climbers, hastily abandoning their designs on the tower (it was to have been an all-night climb), came down again to the "bicycle track", and one of them began to descend to the ground.

Just then the door of the turret banged and a porter came out on to the roof.

Before he came in sight he would have to walk half-way round the Chapel, so they had half a minute in which to make themselves scarce. The second man, deciding he had not time to climb down, slipped over the balustrade and on to the outside of a buttress. The first man hastened his climbing to the point of danger. On the top of the pointed canopy he trusted a stone knob more blindly than he would normally do, and it broke off. He fell twenty-five feet.

By a strange coincidence, he was the person whom such a fall was least likely to hurt. It had long been a theory of his that a climber should know how to fall without hurting himself. In pursuit of this pessimistic ideal, he had been dropping from a height every day for months.

To every labour, its reward. He gathered himself in the air, flexed his knees at the right moment and escaped unscathed.

The second climber, meanwhile, was swinging round the pillar with equal agility each time the porter passed in front of him. He succeeded in escaping notice, and the porter, convinced that they had slipped down the wall like a puff of smoke, went away.

This possession of magic powers which land-lubbers accredit climbers is often astonishing. A friend of ours – usually intelligent – once pointed at the red, unrelieved wall of a prison rising for forty feet without the shadow of a hold anywhere, and asked if it could be climbed. He thought the cracks between some of the bricks were sufficient.

And now for an account of the climb. It appears in the *Rucksack Club Journal*, 1926, from which we will quote:

"St John's Chapel challenges King's in the matter of height, though few would say in beauty, and far overtops all the other college buildings. It is in the shape of an elongated T, with a large square tower rising from the junction of the arms. Three ridges abut this tower at a height of about 80 ft., and from there it rises sheer for another 70 ft. to the balustrade. Fifteen feet above the side ridges, but only nine from the main ridge, a large overhanging ledge completely encircles it. Short square drain-pipes, ending in cast-iron bowls 3 ft. below the overhang, offer a nebulous means of attack from the side ridges. Above the ledge three pairs of louvred windows on each face provide promising going for the next 30 ft. Above that an insignificant diamond-shaped pillar, and the inverted-V mouldings above the windows, end in rosettes below the forbidding overhang of the coping.

"The tower was first attacked by 'Jones' and 'Robinson'. Having first attained the gutter by way of the hall roof, they reached the top of one of the side ridges by climbing the steeply sloping coping at the outer end, of which the topmost rib offers a continuous-grip hand-hold. From the ridge it was easy to swarm up the pipe to the bowl, but the negotiation of the overhang proved exceedingly delicate. It was necessary to work one leg over the serrated top of the bowl, which is only nine inches wide, and flush with the wall, and then to rise to a standing position by aid of a poor handhold on the ledge above. This as it turned out, constituted the *mauvais pas* of the climb. Beyond the edge they did not proceed, as the overhanging heights above appeared at the time completely impassable.

"Circumstances prevented further activity, so that, having heard Jones express the opinion that the top part might go, if surveyed first with a rope from above, some of us decided that an investigation might be worth while. Accordingly we secured, by nefarious means, a dupli-cate key to the staircase which led from the balustrade to the top of the tower. Judge our joy when we discovered that the sloping overhang of the coping could be negotiated quite simply by the aid of some ornamentation on its under side, which proved an efficient hand-hold, so that one could lower oneself sufficiently to grasp the diamond pillar. Once on this, it was tolerably easy to climb down to a small stance on the capital of the pillar between the windows. Thence a sensational step brought the climber underneath the arch, and a circular window above the louvers offered a secure if constricted seat. The tower was ours! All that remained was to climb it!

"But here the difficulties commenced – so, armed with 160 ft. of rope, three of us set out. We decided to make the attempt on the side remote from the court, so as not to arouse dean and porters.

"Arriving at the foot of the stone coping, the rope was donned, and I set off up the 70 degree slope. Jones may have found it 'quite easy', but to us it came as the world's worst sweat; the hand-grip is indeed excellent, though crumbling, but that is all that can possibly be said for it. The second man was so exhausted when he reached the ridge that he almost fell over the other side! The third man gave up half-way and was lowered down. It was obvious that the team was not strong enough to proceed, so, in order not to miss the climb, it was arranged that the other two should lower a rope from the top. Scarcely had they reached the gutter and the rope been thrown down to them, when the beams of a powerful spotlight lit up the Chapel. It was a Robert patrolling Bridge Street. The danger was immediate, for were he to arouse the porters we should be trapped, for the gutter ended against the wall of the tower, and is easily reached by porters by means of a staircase on the court side. For long the circle of light zigzagged here and there over the Chapel, but it failed to pick out the cramped motionless figure which sat shuddering on the sharp ridge. At last the light went out, but not for long. It reappeared directly below, and recommenced its search. But the others had gone, and seizing a favourable opportunity the figure on the ridge resolved itself into human shape, and slithered down the coping at so great a speed that the smell of burning arose from what had once been trousers!

"A few weeks later another attack was made, again with a novice – whom we will call Fisher – a born climber, whose ability to hang on in unpromising situations gave evidence of the true spirit. This time we took the court side, judging porters to be less offensive than Roberts. Once more we found ourselves on the unpleasantly sharp ridge, and at last the drain-pipe rose before us. But the mantelshelf problem of the bowl defeated us utterly and completely; for two hours we sweated and struggled in turn, a wary eye on the Porters' Lodge the while, but all in vain.

"Even assistance offered by Fisher from above only demonstrated the elasticity of 80 ft. of Alpine rope. Crestfallen and annoyed at defeat by what had already been climbed, we retired as dawn was breaking, and set ourselves furiously to think.

"Six months later our thoughts matured into action. The omens were favourable; a bright moon hung in a cloudless sky; the porters on duty were peaceful and fond of their beds; the dean was reported to be sleeping more soundly than usual. Moreover the key had been mislaid, so that there was now no easy way to the top; it was to be all or nothing.

"We had conceived the idea that a stirrup rope might be contrived to supply the absent foot-hold below the bowl. The plan succeeded admirably, and on the second attempt Fisher attained the long-sought ledge. In a few minutes I had joined him, but without the aid of a stirrup the overhang proved as troublesome as ever, and it was only by the skin of my teeth that I avoided using the rope. Together we surveyed the scene from the narrow ledge – above us rose another 50 ft...

"Once more we continued the ascent, certain now that victory would be ours. The louvers proved easy going, and I ensconced myself in a comfortable niche to bring up Fisher. It was only then that we realized the horrible congestion of the situation, which made it impossible to change positions in the niche. Consequently Fisher was forced to make the awkward traverse out to one of the capitals. As he did this move with perfect ease, I thought he might as well proceed. This was a mistake, as he had not done the climb before, and the first move off the capitals is somewhat tricky and very exposed. The first attempt was a failure, so I traversed out to the opposite capital. The position was very delicate, for both of us had to make the traverse unheld; but all was successful, and with Fisher safely ensconced in the niche I scrambled up to the last pitch. (The correct way of tackling this piece would be for the second man to lead up to the niche, and so avoid the change-over.) The rosette at the top of the diamond pillar provided an effective belay for the last movement – the whole climb has an ample sufficiency of belays; and a few minutes later both of us stood on the windy lead flats at the top of the tower…

"The descent was uneventful, though, through a misunderstanding when half-way down the first pitch, I had the discomforting sight of the whole 80 ft. of rope describing a graceful catenary to Fisher, ensconced in the niche below. And if Fisher, careless, fell when descending the louvers, what mattered it, for he was well held, and had not the Chapel tower also fallen?"

The wonderful achievement set out in the foregoing narrative raises some interesting speculations.

First, this climb illustrates better than any other in Cambridge how good climbers will disagree as to the difficulty of a particular piece of climbing. Thus, two climbers who had reached the top of the windows assured us that surmounting the bowl of the pipe was simple. We especially asked them about this particular moment. They did not know each other, neither they nor we had read the foregoing account, yet both were emphatic that surmounting the bowl was easy enough for anyone.

We think we can see the answer here. "Working one leg over the serrated edge of the bowl" sounds most unpleasant. Would it not be easier to work up until the bowl was waist-high and then stretch one hand up? By scrabbling with the feet against the wall this should not be a matter of great strength – indeed, we have done it on other bowls and can affirm that it is quite easy.

On the other hand, the last twenty feet, which had defeated all previous climbers, did not seem to worry unduly the foregoing writer. He merely refers to the "awkward traverse" on to the capitals, and the move off the capitals as "somewhat tricky and very exposed". The last two words are probably a clue as to why so many have failed.

115

As may be seen, the upper part of this climb is tremendously exposed, and anyone making the "sensational step" on to the capitals of the pillar might well wonder if he could get back again. He might also wonder if the lichen-covered stone would crumble under his feet.* And a very severe climb with a 70-ft. drop may unnerve the most steady climber when he knows it has never yet been done. The first man to achieve it had the comfort of having previously done it on a rope, and therefore knowing it to be within his scope.

From now on, knowing it to be possible, climbers should be able to complete the climb without previous exploration. Yet the least that can be said of it is that it is very severe, and should only be tackled by climbers with considerable experience. We counsel enthusiasts to climb the tower and from the ground to the roof on different nights, and those who are more dramatically minded to write their own epitaphs. To any who tackle it, good luck. If their inspiration is strong enough, they will succeed.

---

* In 1932 there occurred an incident amusing to everyone except the unfortunate porter concerned, on this last pitch. A friend of the writer, reaching the top of the tower from the inside, had the idea of climbing down a rope for twenty feet to put a white surplice on one of the corner statues. This he succeeded in doing, and the next morning the authorities were faced with the problem of removing the surplice.

A certain rather plump porter very bravely volunteered to be lowered on a rope, and borrowed a sixty-foot length of alpine rope for the occasion. He detached the surplice from the statue, and then called to be pulled up again.

But to their horror his companions found they could not pull him up again, although they could hold him easily enough, the friction of the stone and his unfortunate weight were too much for their pulling powers. So they secured him to the parapet and went down to find another length of rope. For twenty minutes the wretched man dangled in space in the company of saints and kings, who increased his sense of solitude. At length the new rope arrived, and he was lowered onto the roof below. We have been unable to trace his subsequent history.

CHAPTER TEN

Pembroke

"Trudge, plod away o' the hoof, seek shelter, pack"
Merry Wives, I. 3

"Being nimble-footed, he hath outrun us,
But Moyses and Valerius follow him"
Two Gentlemen of Verona, V. 3

THIS COLLEGE has not received from the photographers the attention it deserves. Human capacity is limited, and in the midst of plenty it is difficult to give adequate attention to everything that is of worth. Go to a fat-stock show and you will see farmers, sated with the sight of prize-winners, giving scarcely a glance to bullocks of the most tremendous girth. Wander through a show-garden, and after half an hour of magnificence you will give perfunctory glances to flowers whose beauty is unrivalled elsewhere. Had Shakespeare written a hundred more plays, you might never have read *Hamlet*. And if you are a climber in Cambridge, you may miss Pembroke.

Writing across a distance of many miles, we can record little of interest to the visitor to Pembroke. There are climbs without number, piled up close together like logs on a fire for the spirit of the eager

The Bridge, Pembroke.

climber to devour, but we have done few of them. Like bumblebees in a jam factory, we have buzzed hither and thither in bewilderment, unable to cope with everything around us. There are more climbs in Pembroke and Emmanuel than are dreamt of in the log-book, Percy.

We will start with the Bridge. This is simply a sort of Roland's Gap in the north wall of the college. Tradition says that in the heroic days of old the Master was feeding with his fellows one day when the meat course was brought in. With a resounding "What, hash again!" the Master brought his spoon down heavily, causing the present breach in the walls. The story is of doubtful origin.

We start up the iron grille of any of the three archways. Without much trouble we get the right foot on to the narrow flange of the arch, with the left foot against the vertical grooves of the pillar to one side (see photograph). At head level is a row of spikes, drooping downwards like a shaggy eyebrow, and these spikes are quite firm. Grasp one of these in each hand.

You can now get higher by stepping backwards up the arch. Then step forwards, on to the ledge at the top of the pillar. By now you are holding the spikes from above. With a careful stretch you can reach the top of the balustrade. You may feel acutely conscious of the possibility of being what the French call *éventré*, but the chances of this are small. No climber's intestine has ever yet been found dangling from these spikes.

As this is sometimes used as a way of climbing in, climbers may perhaps wonder at our including it. We do so without compunction, as it is not as easy as several other ways. A man who can do the Bridge will never be kept out of Pembroke.

A second way of climbing in, palatable only to a seasoned climber, is the north face, running from the Bridge up to the Pembroke Street Porters' Lodge. This can be done at any point along its extent. To facilitate the first few feet, it is perhaps easiest to start just right of the entrance to the college.

The ground-floor windows along this face have stone blocks at the side, over an inch deep. These provide a ladder up to the first ledge, between the ground-floor and the first-floor windows. One can then reach the sill of the window above, and get on to the first ledge.

The window above has two cross-bars, the lower one of which enables one to step on to the sill.

Now comes the first difficulty. The stone crest at the side and top of the windows is out of reach, so there is nothing except the upper

North Face of Pembroke.

cross-bar to help one on to the lower cross-bar, which is hip-high. Both cross-bars are covered in the dust of ages, which makes them soft and slippery to the touch, as though they were covered in oil.

Get a knee on to the lower cross-bar, using half a pull-up and half a press-up on the bar above, avoiding the slippery dust with the fingers by gripping as close to the edge as possible. Your hair is now standing on end. With a forearm on the upper bar and a hand on the crest, things become easier, although the last bit is fairly difficult, the height and the stone pavement below making it unpleasant – or, in technical parlance, "interesting".

Coming down again, we will walk in by the Porters' Lodge, if it be before ten o'clock, and glance round the college from the inside.

There is a multitude of climbs in this, known indifferently as Lodge, or New Court. A number of ominous cracks run haphazard about the face of the building, but the stone is probably safe from a climbing point of view. A porter explained to us that the foundations of the building were inadequate; it is gradually subsiding, although quite new, and cracking as it goes. He also told us – informative fellow – that the name of the college was Pembroke, and Emmanuel was down the street. Because we asked for information, he took us for tourists. We thanked him.

It is not difficult to reach the roof in this court. We selected the north-east corner, and remember little of the climb except the last few feet. Here a broad ledge had to be surmounted without holds above until the bottom of the parapet could be reached. As it was in the corner this was easy, and the first climber, with his back to the corner, reached the roof in peace. The second climber, facing the corner, found himself looking at the ground through a crack in the ledge, reaching to the wall. It was a good tenth of an inch wide, just by his

North Face of Pembroke.

knee. With the memory of the Old Library still fresh in his mind, he wasted little time in joining his companion above. No photographs were taken of this climb.

At the top one can climb up to the ridge of the roof, going up squatting backwards in the corner. The method is to press upwards and outwards against the tiles, using the thumbs only. It would seem that this should press one downwards, and it requires thought to understand how the stresses work to produce the contrary effect.

Coming down from the ridge, it is quite amusing to go along to the western end of the court. This is a very strenuous business of surmounting gable after gable, rising and descending ten feet for every ten feet forward, and will be found exhausting. At the far end, after the corner, the balustrade bridges a gap of about ten feet in space. It can be crossed and exploration pursued, if one be so minded.

Our own party were not so minded. Deciding that they were tired after the ridge and furrow business (which was worse than beagling in a nightmare), they decided to enter the nearest window. It was just too narrow for them, and they wanted help from within to pull them through.

A call to a lighted window below produced the usual Pembroke request to "buzzer off". At length a head appeared, and in a few moments five men were in the room above. Shedding superfluous garments, the two climbers managed to squeeze through.

They were warmly welcomed. Sherry was offered to them, and the traditional Pembroke salutation of a punch on the jaw was conspicuous by its absence. After suitable congratulations on their climb, they were asked if they knew an easy way into the college. The Bridge and such ways were no good; it must be suitable for evening dress. The only easy way had been sealed up the previous term.

Their hosts suddenly became coy, and produced a tin box. There was a fund – it was still in its infancy – for providing a new way in. The visitors contributed their mite, and as the fund reached the sum of five shillings a cheer was raised.

Pleasant and hospitable as were their hosts, they were fine young Englishmen of the best Pembroke type. One of them was in pyjamas; a friend – his best pal – had just poured a pint of beer over his trousers.

What will happen to the fund we cannot say – the idea is good; perhaps a workman will be hired to excavate a tunnel, or a duplicate key will be made. A mason may be paid to scratch away the mortar so that a stone block may be removed and replaced by a cardboard cover. For five shillings a knotted rope or rope ladder could be bought – but why go on with such conjectures? It will probably be used to bribe a porter to leave a side door open.

As we wander down an intricate passage into the next court, we come to Hall. On the left, at the south end, is a chimney of very comfortable width whereby the roof can be reached. It is rather short – about twenty or twenty-five feet – and not very interesting.

In the first court there is at least one method whereby the roof can be reached from the ground. There may be more; our exploration of this court did not last twenty minutes.

In the south-west corner, if memory be faithful, there is a square pipe running up fifteen inches from the corner. With the back against the side wall and the fingers round the pipe, one can place the feet against a vertical ledge, projecting for one inch from the side of the wall. It is not easy, especially as the pipe comes close to the wall at about two-thirds of the way up. The roof behind one is fortunately not very high.

The Climber who went up here had the pleasure of watching the three others dutifully "exploring" round the court. They were all a few feet off the ground, and there was something very comic about the whole affair. He was the least imaginative of the party, but tells us that they reminded him of fleas trying to jump out over the smooth sides of a porcelain bowl. Jump, bump, slither down. For jump, the *élan* with which they started; for bump, the pause to think, and the slithering down was similar but more regulated than that of a flea.

Much more could be written about Pembroke if we had the information. Its stone is good, its climbs legion, and we can thoroughly recommend any night climber to pay a few visits to it. Its hospitality is lavish and sincere, and it breeds those strong, silent Englishmen who suck pipes in the Malayan jungle but do not pass exams.

CHAPTER ELEVEN

Trinity

"Once a warrior very angry
Seized his grandmother, and threw her
Up into the sky at midnight"

Hiawatha

WITH THE Guide-book in our pocket and high expectation in our hearts we go to Trinity, the aristocrat of the college climbing-grounds. King's can offer some more severe climbing, St John's has strong counter attractions in the New Tower and the Bridge of Sighs, the Old Library is a safer romping-ground, but Trinity heads the list. It has everything in its favour. It is more extensive than other colleges, and offers every variety of easy and difficult climbing test. The roof-hiker can wander over many furlongs of roof-tops, alone with his thoughts in an empty world, so near and yet so far from the world of sleeping men below. The climber can take his choice of pipe or pinnacle, or sheer face of solid stone. He knows that the pipes are secure, and the stone sound. He finds spice in the continual round of the night-porter, passing through every court once every quarter of an hour. Or, if he be philosophically minded, he can select a quiet spot, hidden from all eyes, where he can brood over the

Trinity Great Gate.

world below and dream of things to come. No one will disturb him.

Arriving outside the Great Gate as we come from St John's Street or King's Parade, we savour our first anticipatory thrill. It is like seeing the first snow when one goes to Austria, or the tops of the distant Coolins when one motors to Skye. Seen from the ground, the Great Gate is impressive, rising squarely to a height of sixty feet. Half-way up the front face sits King Henry VIII, looking a bit crumbly and holding a gold baton.

A certain climber records that he made a half-hearted attempt to reach the seated monarch, and although he failed he considers it to be perfectly possible. The stone-work on this front face is not safe, unlike the rest of the college, and this makes the ascent unwise as well as severe.

King Henry has probably been reached from the ground several times in the past. The story goes that when the renovators put some scaffolding up the front face, they found the baton to be the leg of a kitchen chair, gilded over. What enterprising man removed the original baton, we do not know. Whether it was a cat-burglar hoping to melt it down for profit, or whether it is guarded as a trophy by a former roof-climber, we cannot tell. But it must have caused many a secret chuckle to the man who effected the substitution.

We cannot climb the Great Gate from the front, so we must tackle it from the side. There are drain-pipes within reach both on the north and on the south, and the roof could be reached by either. The pipes on the north are considerably harder, because they keep close to the wall, so we choose the south.

Surmounting a very broad wall via a window-ledge, we find the pipes, two or three of them, round to the left of the Great Gate. At least one of them is well away from the wall, and in a few feet we are level with the roof, which consists of sloping tiles.

Getting on to this looks difficult, but is quite easy. Round to the right, the vertical wall of the corner turret cuts up through the roof at an angle of forty-five degrees to the gutter. As one edges round this corner one feels more secure, although there is no hand-hold. Lying down, one can reach the lower end of a short drain-pipe, and pull up between two gabled windows on to the edge of the roof.

With an almost inevitable clatter of loose tiles we can go down to the battlement-walk on the far side. Or, if it be a dark night when

Great Gate, Trinity. From roof to top of tower.

silhouettes are blurred, we can straddle along the ridge until we reach the red brick wall of the tower. The pipe is now on our left.

It is an easy pipe, set in an obtuse angle of the wall, whose brick is rough and prevents the feet from slipping. A wire-rope lightning conductor runs down by the pipe and feels safe, but should not be used. There is plenty of room behind the pipe.

As seen from the photograph, the pipe stops well short of the top. A square-cut drainage hole just above the bowl provides a firm finger-hold, although one has to feel inwards for about a foot until one finds it. With the left fore-arm inside this, one can stretch up for the next three or four feet until one reaches the battlement of the tower. The four corner turrets can each be climbed by a short pipe, but they are quite difficult.

The whole climb is very similar to the St John's Main Gate; the second pitch is harder and the first pitch easier than their counterparts.

From here, if the climber be making a circuit of the Great Court, he can go down the north side by a similar pipe. If he would do this circuit, he must have a companion and a short length of rope, or he will not be able to manage it. To get on to the Chapel, the human ladder must be used. For this, one climber supports the other on his shoulders. He then stretches his arms upwards, and keeps the upper man's feet from slipping as he goes up. The rope enables him to follow.

If the circuit of the Great Court is not being made, it is best to descend on the south side. The descent is also easy, and we are back at roof-level surprised at the simplicity of the climb. The Guide sighs over this, but consoles itself as follows: "Old age creeps upon every pipe, and will upon this one in its turn. Then climbers will be forced to use illegal methods – God forbid the firing of rockets or cross-bows, but perhaps the throwing of balls of string from side to side – in order to make their peak; or else give up the Great Court circuit and sigh for the good days of old." Old age is a long time creeping; the pipe is still as good as new.

In photographing the Great Gate, we had an exciting half-hour. It was half-past seven in the evening, and several people were walking about in the Great Court. This meant that the flash was bound to be seen, but that the party had a better chance of mingling with the common herd if any porter should see them. In the dead of night men on nefarious business feel very conspicuous; in the evening, if they are sufficiently hard-boiled, they can talk and joke with their pursuers, unknown and unsuspected. (Burglars, please note.) It is the unexpected that has the best chance of success.

Immediately after the flash, the man with the reflector and the second climber hurried along the battlements, and in through a gabled window farther along. The camera-man waited for No. 1, who arrived as a porter arrived on the ground immediately beneath. The log-book records the incident:

"Looking over the battlements, N.C. and I saw a porter running along below, so there was no time to spare. A man on whose window I had playfully tapped put out his head and said 'Miaw'. The porter looked up, ten yards to the right, but did not see us.

"We popped into the room of the man who had miawed, and found him entertaining half a dozen friends. We had a glass of sherry and explained the situation, promising him a copy of the photo for some magazine. Twice the door opened, and twice I thought we were sunk. We left.

"N.C. now went out of the window on the landing and turned left. This saved me. A porter saw him, as it later transpired, and went along to the room which he entered. And I, walking boldly down the stairs and out towards the fountain, met no one. Had we both walked out, the porter would have been on to us.

"By unbelievable good fortune, there were two doors to the room which he entered. N.C., believing himself fairly safe, was just closing one door when the other opened. He just closed his own door in time, and heard the voice of a porter asking if anyone had climbed in through the window. He hurried out into the court, met me by the fountain and said, 'They're after me'. Rather abruptly, I told him he did not know me, and while he went towards King Edward's Tower I walked out of the Great Gate, meeting no one. The porters were all out looking for us.

"As no one was actually chasing N.C., he was all right, climbing out by…" But that would be telling.

"The man into whose rooms N.C. and I climbed was closely interrogated by the porters. They insisted that they had seen someone climb out of his room. This he stoutly denied; it was the landing next to his room.

"Alec and O'Hara, first away, are to be congratulated on their courage and presence of mind in taking the paraphernalia with them through the teeth of unknown dangers, before the chase was really roused."

Theirs was certainly a remarkable escape. They guessed – correctly – that if they walked out into the court with the suitcase and the reflector they would be caught. If they moved along the battlements, they would be seen and their progress followed. If they went over the ridge of the roof and down to the gutter on the other side there was a sheer drop. There was no easy window from which they could fall. They were trapped, with luggage, on a staircase leading out into the Great Court. Soon porters would be searching every staircase, every room. What then?

In this extremity, without ever having previously studied the environs, they escaped from the college without entering the Great Court, without being seen, without a rope or string, with a bulky reflector and a heavy suitcase.

Men like this would find the rope trick easy.

All this the log-book records – with the explanation, which cannot be recorded here – and continues: "At the Blue Boar we had a drink, patted ourselves on the back, and went off to the Third Court of St John's".

Now comes the real jest. While the photographers spent half the night flashing in St John's, the unflagging Trinity porters continued the hunt. Whether they thought they would return, or had not left, we do not know, but there were four porters looking for them until four o'clock in the morning. And the last of the photographers had left more than six hours previously. We would like to hear what those four porters said to their wives when they arrived home.

We subsequently found that these porters had some grounds for continuing their search. One of our party was staying at the Blue Boar Hotel, which someone discovered, and a plain-clothes detective was set to watch the place at night. It happened to be our meeting-place. He waited until we had gone out, and apprised whomsoever was concerned that we were abroad. Whether he served any colleges other than Trinity we do not know, but that college at least knew when we went out and when we returned. The Great Gate was photographed on a Wednesday. On the Friday we met a friendly policeman who told us about the Blue Boar being watched, and proved his words by telling us at what times we had gone out and returned for three nights. Fortunately, instinct had kept us from going into Trinity since the Great Gate episode.

It was decided that the plain-clothes detective must be shaken off. The man staying at the Blue Boar paid his bill, bade an ostentatious farewell to his friends, and drove away to stay with friends living in Cambridge. Thereafter work continued as before, without the colleges being apprised of our coming on each occasion. Two or three policemen found our change of rendezvous, but faithfully observed our request to keep the knowledge to themselves.

When the hubbub has died down we will return, and continue our exploration of the college. From the Great Gate we travel south, along the battlements, and past a succession of gabled windows, some of them lighted, unless it be very late at night. As you pass them, your silhouette is screened for the whole court to see, but there is no cause for worry. It is the custom of humanity to look at its boots as it walks; we have often proved it.

Some eighty yards or so after turning the corner we come to Queen Elizabeth's Tower, which must be crossed. One can step on to it from the ridge of the roof, but this cannot be reached from the top of a gabled window. A little ingenuity becomes necessary. Choosing a sound tile two or three feet up, place a foot firmly against it. Now spring forward, gaining additional distance with this foot. You can then reach the ledge, and in a few moments are on top of the tower.

Of the four corner turrets, one of us found them very easy, and one quite difficult. Curiously enough, our views were reversed as to the degree of difficulty of the turrets of the Great Gate.

Before going on, it is rather fun to throw things down on passers-by in Trinity Lane. The missiles cannot be seen as they sail downwards, but a direct hit can usually be recognized. This pastime is not dignified, but we repeat, rather fun.

Then on to the end, where the corner causes a short delay. A long stretch upwards can only just reach a leaded, square ledge, on to which one must pull up. This is an energetic scramble, unless one uses a ledge some way out to the right as a foot-hold. One then bids farewell to the Great Court, turns left past the end of Hall until one finds oneself looking down into Nevile's Court. On the opposite side is the Library, a long, rectangular building rising to a height of about fifty feet. We shall come to it later.

At the moment we are concerned with the ascent of Hall. Here the present edition of the Guide quotes from the first edition of 1901:

"The slightly raised coping which edges either end provides the key. Holding its square edges with both hands and placing the feet on the narrow lead gutter, the climber pulls up hand over hand, the tension of the arms keeping the feet from slipping. The stone pilaster on the summit is generally embraced with panting satisfaction, as the height makes the strain upon the muscles considerable. A few moments can well be spared for the view, and few could be insensible to its charms. The distant towers of the Great, New and Nevile's Courts, looming against the dark sky, lit by the flickering lights far below*; the gradations of light and shadow, marked by an occasional moving black speck, seemingly from another world; the sheer wall descending into darkness at his side, the almost invisible barrier that the battlements from which he started seem to make to his terminating in the Court if his arm slips, all contribute to making this esteemed, deservedly, the finest view-point in the college alps."

We have one observation to make.

If the climber lean well forward, he can relieve the strain on his arms by taking all the weight on his feet and simply walking up. As long as he stoops down and holds the coping, pulling perhaps slightly as he does so, he is quite safe. He then arrives at the ridge without tiring. Should he climb up on a rainy night, however, he will have to pull up, and will then have the experience of the Guide.

Once on the ridge, the lantern is on our left. This is a tall, spindly,

---

* Notice this was written before the days of electric light.

lead-and-glass affair, closely resembling the classical conception of a spinster aunt. Rising for twenty or twenty-five feet from the middle of Hall Ridge, it is perhaps the most sensational pinnacle in Trinity, though it is not reckoned a difficult climb. We have not done it – when it fell due we decided we were too unpopular in Trinity – but we have spoken to several who have done it. The prevalent opinion is that it is easy for a tall man, but the shorter the climber, the harder it becomes. A clumsy climber might break some of the glass windows; great care must be taken to avoid this, as they would be difficult to repair. The one thing on which a night climber should pride himself is on leaving no trace of where he has been, and doing no damage. Otherwise he ceases to be a nuisance and becomes a menace.

Coming down again, we proceed to Palisado Corner, at the far end of Hall. Here we can take a good look at the Fourth Court climb before going down to the ground and tackling it from below. The Guide has it in full – we apologize for poaching again, and promise that this is positively the last time we shall quote a climb verbatim:

"*The Fourth Court Climb.* – A lilac bush behind the balustrade may serve for screen, until the light through the frosted glass assures us that we have the climb to ourselves. An easy movement, a lie-back* with the right hand and a press-up with the left, and then an almost similar one with help from the open window, establishes us above the light. From here a broad ledge can just be reached with the hand, and a pull-up on a small subsidiary ledge assists us on to it; the drain-pipe again affording a grateful lie-back hold. This ledge provides the first breathing-space.

"A step then brings us on to the sill of the first-floor window.

---

* The author of the Guide, writing to us, says: "A lie-back hold is back to front and upside-down and, roughly speaking, you pull on it because you can't push".

Trinity, Fourth Court climb. On the first ledge.

Lie-back holds for either hand, left in window and right on the pipe, pull us on to the stone bar of the window; from which the next broad ledge can be reached. A pull-up on to this, with considerable help in steadying from a round drain-pipe above; and then another breather before the last and most fearful pitch.

"One moment of doubt is dispelled by the white upturned faces of the rest of the party, still crouching under the lilac bush far below. A step on to the angle of the serpentine pipe only allows the average man to touch the leaded ledge above. So near and yet so far. Digging the fingers deep into the pipe, we scramble to reach, first the ledge and then a higher wriggle of the serpentine pipe; and quickly disappearing over the balustrade we are on the 'bicycle track'.

"To grasp the ledge above the final pitch requires a reach of 8 ft. 3 ins. from tiptoe. As the majority of people cannot manage this, the climb must be classed as severe, because of its extreme exposure. The leader should not rope for this climb, as the weight of so great a length might drag him off the final pitch."

So speaks the Guide.

We found the first pitch easy, up to the first ledge, although no window was open. Getting on to the first ledge, however, which the Guide dismisses in a line, we found the hardest part of the climb. No first-floor window was open, and somehow the pipe did not help in getting on to it. A press-up on to the ledge was necessary, followed by an extremely delicate piece of balancing. We got on to the ledge, using no hand-holds above until we were standing on it.

At the first attempt we could get no farther, and considered it essential that the first floor window should be open.

Number one retired foiled, but number two found an alternative way up. In the corner, two yards to the right, there is a square pipe.

*Fourth Court Climb, Trinity. The classical route up the pipe to the left
is impossible when the windows by the climber's feet are closed.*

This has finger-room behind it, and enables the climber to reach the second ledge, on to which he can soon manoeuvre himself.

And now the final pitch.

In our opinion, the heroic method adopted by the Guide was unnecessary. The problem, if one be short, is to reach the ledge above, and we suggest as follows:

Face the wall on your right. Take hold of the ledge level with your head, in front of you, and double your left leg under you. Place the foot against the pipe behind, and press with your foot and pull with the arms. Feeling extremely awkward and uncomfortable, you will rise. You can then detach the left hand and grasp the ledge above.

It is a good climb.

Like the Great Gate, it provided the photographers with some fun. Working in the depths of the vacation at two-thirty in the morning, they thought they would be reasonably safe from interference. In this they were wrong.

Just after they had taken the second flash, the door of the passage leading from Nevile's Court to Great Court clanged loudly. Two of the party crouched low behind the balustrade at the foot of the climb. The third jumped over, and dived up the nearest staircase. Though not a climber, he was wearing rubber shoes, and the ring of his steps did not echo round the cloisters. The porter did not see him, but walked all the way round the court, jangling his keys suspiciously. To everyone's horror he then proceeded up the staircase where No. 3 had taken refuge.

On such occasions it is a case of *sauve qui peut*. To be seen is nearly as bad as to be caught, for one's face can be recognized or remembered. If the party scatter in all directions, the pursuit will be perplexed, and each individual fugitive will be harder to locate.

In other words, Nos. 1 and 2 left No. 3 to his fate. Vaulting the balustrade, they made their way out of the college and waited by the car.

They had to wait for some time. No. 3 was an undergraduate from Oxford, whose knowledge of Cambridge and its porters was scanty. When he realized that the minion of authority was coming up his staircase, he records that his hair stood on end. He backed up the stairs and into a garret, whither fortunately the porter did not follow him. What ultimately happened to the trusty servant we cannot say, but No. 3 was some time before he left his hiding-place. Finally he arrived at the car, haggard but triumphant. Usually a cautious driver, on the way home he made the bones of Jehu rattle in their desert grave. Periodically he would erupt into a tremendous burst of song, and the other two quite expected him to stop the car and mount the bonnet, beating his chest gorilla-wise. He had recovered by the next morning.

A present don of the university with a reputation as a great roof-climber has told us an interesting anecdote of the Fourth Court climb. He was wandering round the Trinity roofs alone, when he took it into his head to come down the redoubtable climb. He had never attempted the ascent, and so did not know the details of the holds. A short man, he managed the first pitch, which in going down is severe for a short man, and lowered himself from the second ledge.

With his fingers on a subsidiary ledge two feet lower, and his feet on the cross-bar of the window, he found himself stuck. The window was closed, and he could find no adequate hand-grip to lower himself farther. He did not notice the square pipe to the right, which ends below the ledge, and with his arms already tired after the first pitch, he could not hold on for long. His fingers relaxed, and he fell backwards for twenty or twenty-five feet, injuring his back.

In those days he was an undergraduate of Trinity. On hands and knees, he crawled across the court and up the stairs to his room, only to find that the oak was sported, and he was locked out. So he crawled out again, and along to the Porters' Lodge, where, behind the porter's back, he managed to sneak the key of his room and get away unseen. This would have been a remarkable achievement for an uninjured man: for a newly crippled body it was little short of a miracle. Still crawling, he went back to his room, where he spent the rest of the night. The next day he went to a nursing home, and rang up the college to say he would be away for a week. So ends the tale.

And now, the Library.

We will start with that classic but highly overrated climb, the Trinity Library Chimney. It is to be found at the north-east end of the building, some twenty feet or more from the ground. It can be reached by two iron ladders from the stoke-hole, or in three or four other ways, including a difficult climb from the ground, called Castor and Pollux by the Guide.

A brick chimney-stack rises up to the roof-level of the Library, standing up from the lower roof, gaunt and needle-like, for thirty feet and more. It is between this chimney-stack and the main wall that we ascend. Immediately on our left as we start is a sheer drop into a sort of back-yard.

The right half of the chimney is nearly six inches narrower than the left, and only allows of back-and-knee work. The left half is of an awkward width, but is much easier and quicker than the right.

We recommend having the back to the Library, because the hands can then pull downwards against the corners of the stack, with the flat palms, which assists greatly the action of chimneying in that constricted space. On the other hand, if the climber has his back to the stack he can press downwards with his hands behind his hips. It is a matter for individual preference.

Library Chimney, Trinity.
The climber, with arm raised, can just be seen at the top.

After sixteen feet the chimney widens and becomes easy. At this juncture it is best to turn, with the back to the stack. One can then press without difficulty through the narrow gap made by the wide ledge at roof-level, projecting for two feet towards the stack.

The Guide gives the height of the chimney as thirty-one feet; it seems much less. Two of the photographers, seen on the roof in daylight, reckoned they each got down the chimney in twenty seconds. Certain it is that the first one was down faster than his companion could lower a camera on a string. Wedging their feet, they did not chimney but slid down, without losing control. As one of the two was a Trinity man, his haste may be understood. He changed in a near-by room, and records that as he walked out of college he saw a porter, complete with bowler

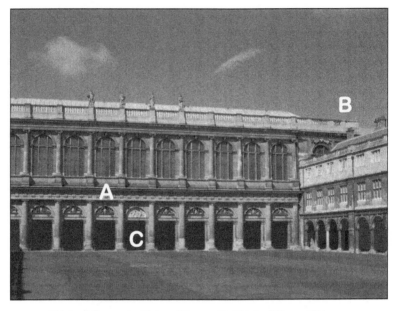

Trinity Library. A: Cloister Terrace; B: Trinity Library Chimney;
C: Foot of Gateway Column climb, on the outside.

hat, walking majestically along the "bicycle track" on the roof of the
north side of Nevile's Court.

The curious thing was that these photographs, taken from the roof
to show a climber in the chimney with the wide-open spaces of the
Master's garden far below him, never came out. On the two or three
occasions that we tried working by daylight the results were always very
under-exposed. The only satisfactory results were by flashlight.

Close by the chimney is the Ornamentation climb. On this we will
not dwell long, as we have not done it. It is reputed to be much easier
than it looks. We know two moderate climbers who have done it several
times, and found it easy; on the other hand a good climber tells us that
it was too difficult for him. So anyone interested must try for himself.

Apparently the difficult part, if it be difficult, is getting from the central boss on to the overhanging ledge immediately above. This is only hearsay, and it is all in the Guide.

Having come down the chimney, we will walk south along a very broad ledge, called the Cloister Terrace, and try the Wet Bobs Traverse on the south end of the building. About half-way up the face it connects the Cloister Terrace with a similar ledge on the other side, known as the River Terrace.

It consists of two ledges, the lower one being about two inches wide. As one stands on this the upper ledge is at about chest-level, and about five inches broad, sloping slightly downwards. It is undercut, and the classical method of effecting the traverse is to slide both hands along the under side of the ledge and shuffle along. Though a considerable strain, this is quite easy.

Easy, but the climber who has experienced the treachery of bad rock is far from easy. The traverse is several yards long, and the undercut hold on which he is pulling with considerable force is only an inch or two thick. Should a piece of rock the size of a small pear break off, he may go spinning down to the ground. In our opinion, he will increase the safety of the traverse by laying one forearm flat on the top of the ledge, using the undercut for the other. In doing this he misses the classical elegance of the climb, but is not left wondering whether the rock is of uniform soundness all the way along. We admire the hardiness of the first man to have tried the classical method.

Walking along the River Terrace, the first thing that happens is that we come to a resounding smack on our nose. Torn between a painful proboscis and relief at not falling to the ground, we turn to investigate the cause. A small iron ring, standing playfully up on end, contorts its hollow features into a grin through our watering eyes. The Guide warned us – perhaps, he too, bumped his nose. We walk along more carefully until a broadening of the ledge indicates that we are over the central gateway. We will now float down to the ground, and try the Gateway Column climb.

The Guide describes this as the "prettiest climb in Trinity". In other words, an absolute stinker. This it certainly is.

We start up the window-bars to the left of the left-hand column. Above the window is a six- or seven-inch ledge on to which it is our first object to ensconce ourselves. When he first tries this a climber may well retire to the ground baffled, reciting "Gunga Din" under his breath in a state of holy awe. But after a little practice, getting on to the ledge becomes quite easy.

Perhaps the easiest way is to face the wall, with the ledge at chest-level. Swing the left leg until it is lying on the ledge, and rolling over we find ourselves lying face downwards on the ledge.

Now follows a nasty piece of balancing, the act of standing up on the ledge. Do not sneeze at this juncture. If you must, you may recite "Gunga Din" in a soft voice, but pay no heed to your companions above or below trying to make you laugh, or you will have to start again.

Next comes the top of the pillar. We were twice foiled by this, and found it much harder than the ledge, but in current opinion it is easier. The Guide, who has nearly ten thousand words to say about climbs in Trinity, dismisses this in the two words "surmounting this". Thus do climbers always differ as to the severity of climbs.

The method – in case you agree with us in finding it difficult – is to grasp the two corners on the left of the pillar. Pull up on these, scratching with your feet against the bare wall. Convert the pull-up to a press-up, and turning round sit down where previously was your left hand. The whole manoeuvre is easier if done quickly.

Trinity Library, Gateway Column Climb. The man in the photograph
is performing the first of three delicate balancing acts.

Gateway Column Climb. This climber is using the wrong method.
He should face the wall and swing his left leg up.

The River Terrace is now just over your head. An iron ring about eight inches in from the corner, with undercut holds below the ledge, makes the surmounting of it fairly easy.

We can now wipe our brow.

As we are already on the outside of the college, we will leave by the back gate – which is locked, but easily surmounted – and walk away along Queen's Road. To reach it, however, we must pass over the river, and take our farewell of Trinity by the Bridge climb. This looks extremely difficult, and is astonishingly easy.

Just above the water-level is a small platform, at the base of the arches on either side. Both the descent and the ascent are equally easy;

Gateway Column Climb. This climber is also wrong. His right hand should be two feet to the right, on the corner. He then pulls up, and turns round to sit on the pillar.

the climber in the photograph is holding the square edge of a crested shield with his left hand, though the effect of the lighting is to make it hardly visible.

One of the earliest adventures of the photographers was on this bridge. A Trinity man had climbed down, and was duly photographed. Hereupon the beam of a torch appeared from the blackness under the Library, and came jogging rapidly towards the bridge. With a low warning to the climber, the rest of the party withdrew towards St John's. The porter stopped on the bridge for some time, scanning the landscape with his torch, but not looking over the side of the bridge. At length he returned whence he had come, and the climber rejoined his fellows. It did not occur to the party until afterwards that it was not

The Bridge, Trinity.

they, but the porter, who was brave. In vile and illegible handwriting it is somewhere recorded that the photographers on several occasions had cause to admire the courage of porters in various colleges.

Incidentally, two of the three Trinity men who were of our party each wanted to tap a porter on the jaw as a means of escape from two rather dire situations. Fortunately they were restrained by wiser and more mature counsel, and the crises were weathered by more constitutional methods. The rules do not permit violence. The climber, like a fox which is hard-pressed, should always have one more trick in his bag.

Sitting on the back gate before going to bed, what climbs have we missed?

We have left out the Great Court circuit, which has some interesting moments. King Edward's Tower we have also not visited, except for a casual look from the ground. (There is an easy pipe five yards to the right of the "eight feet of exposed pipe" which should make King Edward's Tower an easy climb from the ground.) A friend of the writer, who was caught by porters on the roof of the Hall and forbidden to return to Cambridge for three years, told us a good tale about King Edward's Tower. A climber was once in difficulties on this tower when he noticed a rope appearing to dangle for his special benefit. He clutched at it, and the clanging of the great bell above his head nearly caused him to fall to a cobbly death, but the night porter passing below appeared to notice nothing unusual and all was well. On the occasion when the party was caught on the roof of the Hall, they were singing "Porters on the roof-tops, porters on the tiles" to the tune of a well-known refrain. But this is a digression.

Then the Fountain, in the Great Court, the Dip, in the New Court, and Castor and Pollux, in Nevile's Court. The Guide mentions a number of other climbs at which we have not even looked; we have tried to select what seemed to be the major ascents, and then cut out those which could not under existing circumstances be photographed. There is certainly sufficient for climbers of other colleges to pay a few visits to Trinity.

Fortunately for these outsiders, Trinity is an easy college into which to climb. Our own party, who treat climbing-in from a strictly utilitarian point of view, have used six different ways of entry, not counting such climbs as the Gateway Column and the side of the Great Gate. A Trinity don, who in his younger days climbed in by seventeen different ways on seventeen successive nights, was asked how climbing-in could be stopped. He replied: "Encase the college in chromium-plating to a height of fifteen feet, and you may keep out anyone who cannot get hold of a ladder". His advice was not taken.

And so, with a good night's work behind us, we go home to college or lodgings, telling ourselves that perhaps after all we will not attend that nine o'clock lecture to-morrow morning.

CHAPTER TWELVE

King's and Clare

"And they need no candle, neither light of the sun"

Rev. xxii. 5

EVERY PICTURE-LOVER knows that some pictures are better when seen from a distance, while others need to be examined at close quarters to bring out their best effects. The former are roughly drawn, with their commanding features standing out as soon as detail ceases to assert itself. The latter consist almost entirely of detail, delicately joined together, but with no assertive cohesion about them, like flesh without a skeleton. Take Trinity as an example. It has its difficult climbs, but it has taken many years to find them, and they appear rather as emphasized detail than as natural prominences. The Great Gate and the Library Chimney might try to pose as major ascents, but they are only moderately difficult. The Gateway Column, though a difficult and delightful climb, is one which most people would overlook unless forewarned of it. The Fourth Court climb, jostling with the Gateway Column and the Fountain for the honour of the hardest climb in Trinity, has nothing very unique to distinguish it from many other climbs slightly less difficult. Trinity, from afar, looks blurred.

King's and Clare are just the opposite. There is little petty climbing in them, no interesting rambling for the roof-hiker, except perhaps the roofs round Webb's Court in King's. Petty detail is lacking, and five or six severe climbs stand out, stark and challenging. These are the Chapel, Porters' lodge and Chetwynd Chimney in King's, and the Corner and Ladder climbs in Clare. Before doing these, we will look round to see what we can find in the way of other climbs.

Going round the first court of King's, we find a buttress on the King's Parade side of Hall, seeming to make an easy chimney with the main wall. Several climbers have come to us independently and told us of this chimney, announcing their discovery with the zeal of pioneers. But it is too narrow. A Tom Thumb might struggle up, and steal a march on those of more normal proportions, but the average man could not do so.

Proceeding towards the river, we come to Gibb's building on our right. An isolated and rectangular block rising to a height of fifty feet, it appears to offer no possibility of a climb. Close scrutiny, however, will reveal a possible way of reaching the roof. So far as we know it has never been exploited, and as we ourselves have not attempted it we will omit it altogether. This will give climbers the pleasure of looking for it; it is very severe.

A half-minute climb can be made up to the top of the pillars of the central archway of this building. With the back against a pillar, the feet walk up the slots opposite. At the top, we are told, one may slip through to the side of the pillar away from the arch, on to a ledge at the side and so on to the massive sloping terrace above.

A certain Canadian up at King's was once obsessed with an idea about Gibb's. This was to introduce some goats on to the roof. Climbing was not necessary, but the creatures would have to be carried through

Central Archway, Gibbs. The idea is to get round on to the top of the archway.

the room of a sleeping don and through a trap-door to the roof. The vision of a troupe of porters coaxing bearded animals to come off a roof-top appealed to his imagination. As we have said, it was not a mere fantasy, but an obsession.

With an English friend he drove round the countryside, casting longing eyes at the goats tethered by the verge. He made enquiries as to whether it would be cruel to chloroform a goat; he planned a scheme of smuggling the animals into college in a punt, and had fertile ideas about Doping the Don, or enticing him from his rooms for the night.

But it never went further. He was more a man of thought than a man of action. Like a rocket which hisses loudly and then decides not to leave the ground, the idea fizzled out. It was followed by plans to flood the underground passage known as the Drain, to let off fireworks from the battlements of every building in the front court, to release a porker on the lawn during a May Week Ball, and to inflict the college with five hundred living rabbits or twice as many rats (for which a smoke screen was to be used). None of these schemes ever came off, but they afforded their originator many happy hours. With a smile on his face and nonsense in his heart, he is now back in Canada, where he is probably putting toads in his grandfather's boots for want of something better to do. Everyone liked him.*

Wandering down as far as the river, we find nothing to climb except some bleak pipes on Bodley's building. These have occasionally been

---

* The tale of the college crocuses is sometimes attributed to this man. We cannot vouch for his responsibility, though the tale itself is true enough. Wishing to embellish the grass of the lawns, the college ordered a consignment of crocus bulbs. The offer of some undergraduates to plant them was graciously accepted, and the self-appointed gardeners set to work. The task was completed, and like most of such tasks forgotten. For months nothing happened. Then came the early spring, and little heads began to peep above the ground. In letters large and for the world to see there grew out of the ground the exaltation "Bother the Dean", or words to that effect, passing from green suspicion to golden certainty. Of course, this tale has nothing to do with climbing.

climbed, and a friend of ours was once suspended half-way up one of them for twenty-five minutes while the tutor and the junior dean chatted on the grass below; but they offer nothing different from scores of other bleak pipes. So we will return and go up on to the roof of Webb's.

An amusing hour can quite well be spent up here. Over the Kitchen is a sort of cupola with a ball on top which can be climbed by a direct pull-up. There is an intricate maze of roof-levels which can be explored by those who so wish. On the south side are some chimney-stacks on to which one may pull up with a scramble. The only occasion we have visited the roof of this court was over two years ago, when we started from outside the college in King's Lane.

The Kitchen office is close to the cupola. If its window is open (as it was on that occasion) one can wander through the Kitchen quarters and the Buttery and learn much of interest about preparing food for the multitude.

Leaving by a ground-floor Buttery window, we will go to Queen's Road and approach Clare from over the river to tackle the easiest of our five climbs.

The back gate is easily surmounted, though a hasty climber may prick his foot on the spikes four feet up, which are deceptively sharp. Just before the bridge there are some tricky spiked iron railings to negotiate. Then softly along the gravel path, until we are under the gate of the building. We believe that the Master's Lodge is on either side of this.

The climb before us is the Clare Ladder.

The method we adopted was to climb the bars of the iron gate as high as possible. There is then a ledge on the left with ample room for a foot. A small ledge two and a half feet above this affords a good hand-hold, and it is possible to leave the grill.

Clare, the Ladder Climb.

Harder than it looks, as the square pipe does not help, being close to the wall.

A rather clumsy traverse now takes place round the semi-circular pillar, and one gets on to the ladder proper. This consists of narrow slots in the stone, in which a rubber shoe does not feel safe, owing to their small size.

One can rest comfortably on the broad ledge above the gate, and then on to the most difficult bit.

There is a square drain-pipe round to the left which provides scant assistance, as in only one place can one get fingers behind it. However, it helps a little. One more or less has to trust to the ladder of narrow slots.

Soon one can grasp a ledge, and from now on it is easier. The building drops back a few inches to the left of the ladder, and the ledge projects sideways, so that one can get one's fingers behind (see photograph, just below the climber's right foot). It does not feel too safe, but at one moment it bore a climber's whole weight. This was bad climbing.

The last fifteen feet are easier. The bowl of the pipe is not far above the climber's head, and once he has a hand on this he can soon get to the parapet on the left.

The descent is nearly as difficult as the ascent.

We first read of this climb in a series of articles entitled "Alpine Sports in Cambridge", published anonymously in the *Cambridge Review* in 1924. We have done several of the climbs described in these articles, but this was the only one of which we should not otherwise have known.

The second of our five climbs is the south-east corner of Clare, abutting on to King's. The climb starts twenty yards from the foot of the Chapel.

It is a deceptive climb. On the exposed corner of a building, and with three pitches of seven feet with no foot-hold and no hand-holds

South-east corner of Clare.
Note the scratches of previous climbers above the present climber.

except two vertical ledges, it appears at first sight to be impossible. In reality it is not too bad. A little determination and reasonable tummy muscles are more important in this case than technical skill.

The clue to the climb are the vertical ledges two feet to each side, where the building drops back a few inches from the corner-stone. These prevent the climber from falling away from the building.

The horizontal ledges are in groups of three, a foot separating the lower two, and nearly two feet the upper two. The middle one is quite broad, so that one can traverse on it along the whole face of the building.

Reaching the bottom ledge from a ledge three feet from the ground, pull up until you can reach the middle ledge, on which you must also pull up. As soon as possible, get both feet on to the bottom ledge. To do this, the vertical ledges may help, holding them above the top horizontal ledge. Standing on the bottom ledge, you can walk up on to the top ledge, sliding the hands up the vertical ledges.

You are now on the second seven-foot pitch. It is exactly the same as the first, only about twelve feet higher. The third is the same as the second, and by now you may be feeling tired. After the third pull-up you are on the roof. Coming down is easier, though it is not too pleasant having to keep lowering oneself to arm's length.

This climb is interesting in that the arms play a more important part than the legs. Seldom does a climber have to do a straight pull-up, yet here he must do several, since there is not the scratch of a foot-hold to help him on the three seven-foot pitches. The "Alpine Sports in Cambridge" series also contains this climb, though we first heard of it elsewhere. There was a Kingsman who considered this his pet climb; he used to go up to the first or second ledge once or twice a week and traverse along the face of the building.

South-east corner of Clare.

King's Porters' Lodge.

An alternative way up this climb is to be found five yards to the left. This is up the right-hand side of the nearest window but one. The climbing is practically identical, except that the vertical ledges are only eighteen inches apart, and parallel to each other instead of at right angles. This makes it slightly harder. The hold is a flat friction-hold on the flat ledges between the two hands, known in technical parlance, we believe, as a Thank-God hold.

We have now reached the roof of Clare by two routes; for the insatiate climber there is a third, whereby the roof of both Clare and

163

King's Porters' Lodge. Ground to roof.

Trinity Hall can be reached. This is the narrow passage half-way between Trinity Hall Porters' Lodge and the King's north gate.

Leading along between two high walls, it is of ideal width for chimneying. Some high and rather forlorn spikes are near the road, but these offer no serious difficulty. The walls on both sides are very smooth, and some climbers might prefer to go up in bare feet. We have not been up this chimney, but know it to have been climbed.

Leaving this chimney and also Clare, we will go to King's and start the heavy stuff. The Chapel we will leave to another chapter, and tackle the Porters' Lodge.

Porters' Lodge. The clock face.

The ascent of this easy-looking building has been attempted by many climbers with monotonous lack of success. Though not so exposed, the climbing is considerably more severe than that on the Chapel, and as far as we know the unroped ascent has only once been achieved.

From the ground to the roof is easy. A pipe runs down in a corner on the street side, to the right of the gate. The only danger is that it runs close to a porter's window, and he is liable to wake up. On two occasions we have awakened a porter when coming down this pipe.

On the roof it will be seen that the tower rises from a sloping inner roof of slates. One starts up some clover-leaf air holes and quickly up until the head is level with the clock face. Each of the hours on this face is marked by a stone wedge, unsatisfactory as a hand-hold but the best one can have.

At this point one begins to appreciate the unpleasantness of the climb. The holds are so inadequate that one cannot lean outwards; one must keep as close to the building as a barnacle. For on a wedge with the tongue pointing outwards one can pull downwards, but not outwards. Further, one must grip very tightly to counteract the inadequacy of the hold.

The result is that one tires very quickly. Unless one can very soon reach the ledge above, one must come down again for a rest.

With an arm round the pillar one may try to use a similar method to that which is used on the Chapel to surmount the first overhang. There is no incut edge for the fingers on the far side, however, and one must grasp one of the hour knobs on the far side. It is difficult to get higher than the last foot-hold below the clock – perhaps a knee on the six o'clock is the easiest way.

With a hand at last on the ledge above we can stand by the fleur-de-lis and take a rest.

Now comes the Onion.

Ribs of stone run up this, and bring the climber up to the base of the needle. We will quote a few words from the man who achieved the climb.

"Climbing up the Onion was easy, though the stone is crumbly, and where it straightens up I had to put my arms around it in the affectionate way I had seen in use on the lamented Amelia (see below); then there is another arm-pull to the lower of the two ridges round the turret, yet another to the higher, and here tragically my arms gave out. As the place is extremely exposed, I came down; and much to my surprise was able to get down over the overhang without falling. Modestly, I consider this to be a quite remarkable feat, and as I cannot remember how I did it, must conclude that my fear of falling off was too strong for gravity; certainly I have never before hung on to precarious hand-holds with such a leech-like tenacity."

The above climber was graciously repeating his effort for the camera when a misfortune occurred. The Inefficient Photographer* was looking at the flashlight, and pressing various knobs and buttons to see what would happen. The bulbs, tiring of this familiarity, flashed off in his face, blinding him for the rest of the night and part of the next day. They were the last three bulbs, and the climber, heaving a sigh of relief, came down and took the first boat leaving England.

In his absence two other climbers tried one night to reach the top, but failed.

One of the photographers, not himself a climber, fell off below the clock face and landed on his back on the slates. It was only a few feet, and he did not hurt himself, but he cracked some slates which had to be

---

* A generic rather than a specific name.

King's, Chetwynd Crack. This is severe. There are two chockstones,
just above each climber, making formidable overhangs.

replaced. This cost the college three pounds. The news reached us that the head porter attributed this to the clumsiness of some builders some months previously. In pursuance of their no-damage policy, the photographers sent an anonymous letter with three pounds, entitled "conscience money". The bursar must have been considerably surprised.

On three successive occasions climbers on the Porters' lodge betrayed themselves while on the roof. On the first occasion two Kingsmen were concerned, and they got away comfortably. On the second, an alien party was involved, and had difficulty in escaping. With a porter on the ground and a porter on the roof, one of them was forced to drop from the ivy-covered screens at the side of the Lodge. He was not hurt, and with the elder of the two porters on the ground, made good his escape.

The third occasion was mildly dramatic. Another two Kingsmen were involved, and to be seen was to be recognized.

The first climber rattled the pipe, and a night-capped head appeared at the window. There was a bellow of "Police!" which No. 2, still on the roof, did not like. He slipped down the pipe quickly and inelegantly, and bending down so as not to be recognized, pounded away in bare feet. The policeman was at the far end of his beat, and all was well.

In our undergraduate days, before we realized the difficulty of the Lodge climb, we once wanted to adorn the pinnacle with a bust such as may be seen in a milliner's shop. Walking into a large store at lunch-time one Saturday, we asked for a female torso. The lady behind the counter astutely sent for the manager, who came up obviously expecting to have to deal tactfully with a lunatic. At an almost prohibitive cost a bust was procured, and was solemnly christened Amelia. She was a companionable maiden, and lived through some exciting times; but alas! She was never destined to look down on the world from a college pinnacle. Discarded and forgotten, she is languishing in a dusty attic; a butterfly is hibernating on her breast.

Lastly the Chetwynd Chimney.

This looks easy enough, and perhaps it is; but none of the photographers has found it so. To us it seems very severe, and as one climbs it is difficult to forget the stone paving-stones below.

Start up the chimney facing the reading-room window. With back-and-knee work, a press-up with the right hand on the middle ledge of the window, and a wriggle, you can stand up on the ledge.

Now turn right round in the chimney, using the square drain-pipe to prevent yourself from falling outwards. In the wall whose length you are facing is a window, arched over with a sloping projecting flange. Step on to this with one leg.

This enables you to get considerably higher, and you can comfortably reach the iron binding six inches below the overhang. This offers a good end-joint finger-grip, but no more.

You can soon get a moderate grip on the first overhang, and half pulling up and half chimneying, you can get over. A crested shield away to the left and higher than the overhang may help.

The second overhang is even more formidable. It involves going out a foot or two on to the window ledge on the left. In summer it is cloaked in heavy vegetation. Only one of our party has succeeded in achieving the whole climb; three have tried.

Anyone who desires an evening of roof-hiking without the preliminary climbing can get out from the top window above the second overhang. He can try a little mild climbing up the twin pinnacles of Hall. The stone is not too safe; when we climbed one of them, a large piece of stone broke off and clattered noisily down the slates.

And now the Chapel. To climbers the Chapel is a building with a history, and although we have unearthed but few of its secrets, a little has come to light. We have no crystal to amplify this light, no magic mirror to reflect the vanished happenings of the past. Epics may have escaped our notice, tremendous deeds of valour dismissed in a line for want of further information. But what little we have found we will record.

CHAPTER THIRTEEN

The Chapel

"Let not thy voice be heard among us,

lest angry Fellows run upon thee"

Judges xviii. 25 (A.V.)

THERE IS probably no building in the world which has aroused such interest among climbers as King's Chapel. Many men, not otherwise interested in night climbing, make it their ambition to climb it, and all save the very few are disappointed. Towering vertically for a hundred and sixty feet, it was until the New Library was built the tallest building in Cambridge. Tourists disagree as to its architectural beauties, some saying it is too long, but climbers always look at it with awe and reverence. It has a fascination about it which will not let the mind rest. The severity of its aspect is a challenge, a coaxing invitation one minute and a stern rebuff the next. It is possible to grow to love the Chapel, seeing it reflected in every face, hearing the singing of its pinnacles in every storm of wind, thinking of it many times during the day and dreaming of it by night, having only to cast back to it to return to a higher world of thought and feeling.

Whose was the privilege to have first climbed it? We have been

King's Chapel.

unable to discover, although there are indications which enable one to guess at an approximate date.

The college was founded in 1441 by the pious Henry VI, in the midst of turbulent times. The history of those days is somewhat scant, and the chroniclers saved their vellum to record the narrative of battles and campaigns. Is there a likelihood that any adventurer left his gauntlet or his vizor on the top to woo his lady love? Did the White Rose of York or the Red Rose of Lancaster grow on the top of the pinnacles? We think not.

Benjamin Franklin invented the lightning-conductor (or lightning-rod, as he preferred to call it) in 1752. It is probable that soon after that date the first lightning-rod was affixed to the Chapel. Running down the face of the building, it was put in the most inconspicuous place, which by good fortune was the place most suited to help the climber. In our opinion, it was soon after the installation of the lightning-rod that the Chapel was first climbed. The technical reasons for this view will be explained later.

One support for this proposition is a tantalizing peep into the past which we are not able to investigate further. Some years ago a coin was found on the ledge twenty feet below the pinnacle, and the date on the coin was 1760.

Who left it there? Was he an isolated crank who wandered about in the night and did strange things, or was he one of a band of enthusiasts? Has the tradition of climbing the Chapel persisted ever since, or did it slumber for a hundred and fifty years, to awaken in the present century? We do not know. But that coin speaks to the imagination.

The next instance of a climb up the Chapel that we can discover was that of a don during the war. It was done openly in daylight, and was in some way connected with the said don's abstention from military service. Whether it was to prove that pacifists were not cowards, or to prove to the doctors that he was medically fit to fight, we do not know. He is still alive and in residence at the moment of writing, but one cannot pry too closely into the hilarious past of an old man.

Between then and 1932 there were several climbs, about which we have been able to find out little. Some naval men left a bicycle on top shortly after the war; a piece of gown once appeared. In 1922 two men from St John's, climbing on Clare or Trinity Hall, heard a party led by a Kingsman climbing the Chapel. This particular Kingsman tells us that he believes his to have been the first ascent of the pinnacles. The next night they went along themselves, starting on opposite sides of the building and meeting on the roof after twenty minutes. They did not try the pinnacles, but one of them climbed the north-east pinnacle at eleven-thirty the next morning.

Then there is the tale about a certain undergraduate of King's. As we heard it, he determined to climb to the roof of the Chapel without using the conductor. For three months he went along with a companion every night to practise, going a little higher each week. When the time came, he led the way up and lowered a rope to his friend, who returned the favour by roping him down and going down second, so that each went the length of the chimney without a rope. After he had received a fellowship he used to say that it was given to him because of this feat.

In 1932 the Chapel was climbed on two successive nights. On the first, two climbers affixed an umbrella to one of the pinnacles. They took a rope, and a ten-foot stick with a hook on the end, to belay the rope over the projections above the climber. The rope was paid out from inside the turret; the stick was never used.

On the way home they met another climber, who had watched the performance from the roofs of Trinity. Upset at missing the fun, he persuaded one of them to go up again, and they decorated the other pinnacle at the same end with an umbrella stolen from Trinity. The next morning the porters took a young man who possessed a shot-gun up on to the roof, and the offending umbrellas were shot down. A considerable amount of publicity attended this exploit, even finding its way into the correspondence columns of *The Times*.

But one group of climbers was not pleased to see the new orna-mentations on the Chapel. This group had planned an assault of the

Chapel, and now found itself forestalled. So armed with money and grim faces they went off and bought two Union Jacks. These were duly affixed over the umbrella stumps during the night watches, and in the morning the dean again sought out the young man with the gun, to send him up with the porters. The young man, known to his friends as "The Admiral", demurred against firing upon the British Flag. The dean, with the steeplejack's fee of twenty pounds in his mind, tried to uproot these feudal scruples, but The Admiral was loyal to the core. He drew himself up to his full height.

"Sir," he said, "I cannot shoot upon the Union Jack."

For self-conscious drama this scene must have rivalled the famous meeting between Stanley and Livingstone. The steeplejacks were sent up from the roof, and the flags were brought down.

The authorities professed themselves very worried about the safety of young men who could expose themselves to such appalling risks, and the lightning-rod was moved so as to be of no further help to climbers. There was, indeed, a rumour that one of the climbers had lost his nerve on the roof and had practically to be lowered to the ground. This was probably utterly without foundation.

Certain it is that at least one of these parties was troubled with crumbling stone-work near the top, hand-holds coming off at inconvenient moments. The Chapel began to acquire a sinister reputation, and climbers said that anyone who reached the pinnacles would be in terrible danger from the soft stone. The Chapel declined in popularity.

But such a stupendous building could not remain unpopular for long. In a short time, attempts were being made to climb it again. Some of the best climbers in Cambridge prowled beneath its disdainful walls, but with no prospect of success. Without the lightning-rod, the Chapel was proclaimed to be impossible.

But it was nearly conquered, by a subterfuge, in 1934. Three conspirators entered the Chapel one afternoon in October, and one asked to go on the roof to "see the view". The Chapel clerk gave him the key, and the others drew him away from the turret door to look at the date on a tombstone.

A fourth conspirator entered the Chapel two minutes later, with an old mackintosh on his arm. Inside that mackintosh was a hundred-foot rope.

Seeing that Nos. 2 and 3 had manoeuvred the Chapel clerk to the far end of the Chapel, No. 4 slipped across and into the turret where there is a spiral staircase. After a farewell in which the traditional handshake was omitted, No. 1 returned, and the verger locked the door with No. 4 inside.

For two hours he waited, and he passed most of the time sleeping with the rope as a pillow. It would have been embarrassing had another visitor gone up in the meantime to see the view. But this did not happen, and he awoke with a start to find it was dark, with the last splashes of the sunset showing through a slotted Norman window. He walked along the leads, tied the rope to the parapet, and looked down.

It was pretty formidable. He threw the mackintosh over, and watched it open out and billow down through seemingly interminable space. The bottom of the rope was not touching the ground. Below and on the right, a lamp-post was shining cheerlessly in King's Parade.

There was one difficulty which had not been previously considered. The rope could not be fixed nearer than a yard to the side of the chimney. This meant that the climber must start off on the rope alone, or in the chimney without the rope. For if he got into the chimney and tried to use the rope, it would pull him outwards. He elected to start off down the rope, trusting to his ability to manoeuvre himself into the chimney lower down. It was not too cheerful a prospect, and he records that he had an earnest exchange of views with the stars above before slipping over the edge.

As the roof-level slipped past his chest, past his head and then out of reach, he experienced his first difficulty. The rope, true alpine hemp, was too thin to grip with his legs. He descended rapidly hand over hand for a dozen feet, coiled the rope round one foot with the other, and rested as much as the situation allowed. He then freed his foot, and tried to swing into the chimney. But it was useless, either his feet or his body struck first, and bounced out again. Thus he wasted much time and strength. He coiled the rope round his foot and took another rest. By this time he was unpleasantly aware that there were still over seventy feet between himself and the ground; there remained little chance of his reaching the ground in safety.

By a curious perversity, the human mind refuses to behave itself on the occasions when it should be intensely dramatic. It was so now; the climber suddenly forgot his fears in a smile. The choir had chosen this precise moment to start the Nunc Dimittis.

After one more attempt, ten feet lower down, to get into the chimney, he decided to complete the descent hand over hand. Forty feet from the ground the strength of his arms gave out, leaving him to make a rapid decision between breaking his neck or burning his fingers. He burnt his fingers, and for six weeks his hands were in bandages.

This happened soon after six o'clock. The rest of the party, not minded to be pulled out of the chimney by the rope, deferred their attempt, and the rope was impounded by the college authorities, being used to this day as a bell-rope in the Chapel. The dean of the delinquent's college was minded to send him down, but a kindly tutor intervened, and fortunately for the man concerned had the final word. The delinquent now collects butterflies.

Thereafter, the college made every visitor to the roof write his name in a book and pay a toll of sixpence.

But the climbers had their counter-move ready. A certain George (now a schoolmaster in Kenya and a mile record-breaker) offered to help at this stage. Tall and stooping, and steadfastly carrying an umbrella through drought and heat-wave, he often used to call on the writer. After a slight pretence at conversation which deceived no-one, he would always gravitate to the piano to our tattered old copy of Beethoven. We always liked to listen to him, not because of the abominable way in which he leaned forward and glared at the music, and not because of his discords, which were atrocious, but because it was George.

This George concealed a hammer in his spacious trousers and a cake of soap in his pocket. Obtaining the key from the verger on payment of sixpence, he started up the spiral staircase. In the darkness half-way up he laid the soap on a stone step, laid the key on the soap, and dealt it a shrewd blow with the hammer. The soap crumbled into twenty pieces.

Returning the next day with some softer soap George obtained an impression of the key, or rather two impressions, sideways and endways. This was all that was needed to make a duplicate impression of the key.

With rising hopes of success, one of the climbers was then despatched on a special visit to London. He called on a criminal locksmith in the neighbourhood of Camomile Street, and had a key made from the impressions on the soap. The key was four inches long, but not long enough for the stout oaken door to the turret. The locksmith was revisited, and lengthened the key by two inches. George returned to the Chapel and tried the key on the turret door. It fitted, and the door opened.

This, however, was placing the cart before the horse. The climbers had the key to the turret, but not to the Chapel.

Nothing can be done without trying. One night one of them woke up at 4 a.m., slipped out of bed, dressed, and visited the Chapel. He took with him a piece of wire and a torch. The idea occurred to him that it might be possible to open the lock with the wire. Thus do criminal locksmiths suggest ideas!

He pressed slightly on the door and it gave way to his touch. *Mirabile dictu!* It was open. He stepped into the scented darkness within.

Here, he records, he was faced with an urgent dilemma. The door was open, presumably by accident, and the opportunity might never occur again. What should he do?

Of his climbing associates, one was in Caius, two in Pembroke, and two in Emmanuel. It was after four o'clock, and there was no time to rally the clan. They might even show a certain reluctance to be pulled from their beds at four-thirty in the morning to dither skywards. So he returned to bed. A new hope lulled him ecstatically to sleep, and he waited for the next night.

Twice more he visited the Chapel alone, and each time the door was open. He dropped in casually at the Porters' Lodge the next day and in the course of conversation asked a simple question.

"Why is there an iron grid in front of the Chapel door? An iron lock and oak door should be sufficient."

"Ah yes, but you see, sir, the Chapel door is never locked. We lock the grid, instead, so that the organ scholar and others can have a key."

So that was it.

The clan gathered like earwigs round an orange-peel. The two Emmanuel men had dropped out, but the four remaining men trooped up to the roof at the first opportunity. All is not orange-peel that glistens, however.

After they had groped their way up the spiral staircase in single file, they stepped out on to the roof and proceeded to the far end. Here Hugh, of Caius, was called into action. He was at that time reputed, in a vague and shadowy way, to be the best rock-climber in Cambridge. The happy idea was that Hugh should climb up and lower a rope to the less elegant members of the party. Hugh started up, and everyone was pleasantly thrilled. Everyone was confident of success.

But at the first overhang he stopped. With five feet without a hand-hold, the overhang was more than he could manage. By a magnificent feat of balancing, he got his hand to within a foot of the next hand-hold above, but there he stopped. He came down again. If someone would come up with him so that he could stand on their shoulders – and he looked meaningly around.

He was a small light man, but was too heavy for anyone to take his weight while hanging on to a vertical face. The rest of the party tried, but none could reach as far up as Hugh by nearly a foot. It was Hugh's misfortune that he did not discover the inside edge of the corner pillar, which could be used for chimneying between the centre of the face.

Hugh having failed, the turret was declared unclimbable. How, then, had previous parties succeeded? The obvious answer seemed, the lightning-conductor. Unfortunately, there was at this time a rumour current among climbers that the staples of the conductor had been loosened to prevent future ascents of the Chapel. No one cared to traverse round and test the conductor, and the party retired, foiled.

The component parts of a sweep's rod were then brought into play. The object was to get a rope over the crenellated parapet, forty feet above the roof. But the rod was so supple that it bent under its own weight, and was discarded.

There seemed only one thing to do, namely, to throw a string over the parapet, and haul the rope up. A tennis-ball was tied in a handkerchief and the attempt made.

The aperture to be aimed at was only six inches wide, forty feet up, and the thrower had to stand on a roof sloping at an awkward angle. The string had to be lain loosely on the roof, so as to offer the minimum impediment to the flight of the ball. Then someone would stand on it. Or the thrower would catch the string on a button so that the ball swung round and hit him in the face. Or the string got tangled into heavy knots, or a gust of wind came at the wrong moment. The slightest breeze had its effect, and the thrower had to be accurate to within six inches. Every time he missed, the tennis-ball had to be hauled up from somewhere near the ground. With all their difficulties, the climbers spent half an hour between each throw. Fumbling in the dark as they were, on the *qui vive* for policemen in the street below, their chance of success seemed small. They were now to lose Hugh.

Brilliant climber though he was, Hugh suffered from roof-climber's claustrophobia. He argued that, if they made a noise and were unlucky, they would be discovered, and would have to descend the spiral staircase into the arms of a porter. As a result, he left the Chapel clan and indulged in climbs that were equally thrilling but less glorious. Of the original six, three were now left.

This was perhaps the darkest hour, in which ultimate failure began to appear as a possibility. No one would have admitted this, however, and before long one of the party had an idea which seemed feasible.

He was an archer. What more simple, than to shoot arrows over the parapet? He knew the accuracy of the bow, how it was comparatively easy to hit a post card fifty feet away. He pierced the nock end of an arrow with a hot iron, threaded string through it and made experiments near Grantchester. It worked.

Full of renewed hope, the party revisited the roof with balls of string, a bow, arrows, a Union Jack, torch, and various small impedimenta. Climbing over the iron grid outside the main entrance, always a risky business with a college lamp-post fifteen feet away, was accomplished with unavoidable janglings. They clanked their way up the pitch blackness of the spiral staircase, and out on to the roof. On half a dozen nights they went on to the roof, but could not succeed in making the string stay up. Once, indeed, they thought they had succeeded, and began to haul the rope up, but somehow it managed to fall down again.

Looking back, it was certainly rather comic. First, one of the party would walk up and down laying out hundreds of feet of string on the roof, taking great care to avoid tangles. At length, with everything ready, the archer would nock the arrow and draw the bow. This was the big moment. With the others waiting anxiously on either side of him, he would carefully aim and release the arrow. If the string were not twisted round someone's coat button, the arrow would vanish upwards into the blackness above the pinnacle. For about three seconds length after length of string could be seen in the lamplight hurtling upwards from the roof, and then came a pause, during which everyone wondered if the shot had been successful. If it had not broken away the arrow was then hauled up, and in due course the process was repeated.

They record that February in 1935 was a cold month. On one night they were on the roof for two hours in a howling east wind, with the temperature several degrees below freezing. They wore no gloves. When it was time to go they called the look-out man, but received no answer. He had congealed into a coma.

Going down the staircase was hair-raising on one occasion, when steps were heard coming up. The four climbers nearly died of fright before deciding that it was only the echo of their own footsteps reverberating from below.

On another occasion the archer, going to the far side of the Chapel to find an arrow that had broken the string, saw a light in the Chapel. The time was 4.30 a.m. Again the clan had the Glen Coe feeling, though the next day our Diplomatic Correspondent, acting according to his own methods, ascertained the cause. A light had been left on in a side Chapel.

Being left with no alternative, the party admitted defeat, bade a courteous farewell to the roof-tops, and settled down to a few hours' work a day for the June exams. We then pass on to the successful assault of June.

The Tripos over, two of the party were celebrating in the usual manner. As they ran down Pembroke Street towards Emmanuel, one of them turned aside and playfully glided up the face of the Law Schools. He achieved this by holding one of the pillars with his hands and using wayside knobs as foot-holds. In a flash it occurred to him what afterwards seemed blindingly obvious. Use the pillar to surmount the two overhangs.

It was arranged that Charles, of Pembroke, should bring Bill, also of Pembroke, the next night at midnight. Alas! Charles made the promise glibly, and forgot all about it.

For an hour No. 1 waited. By good fortune an excellent climber was passing the evening with him, and this man was empanelled as No. 4.

They each attacked a turret, and the theory evolved on the face of the Law Schools was proved to be correct. With considerable trepidation, No. 1 surmounted the two overhangs and stood on the parapet.

But he had forgotten the flag.

While No. 4 went off to collect this, No. 1 collected a number of oddments – about a dozen arrows, hundreds of yards of string, tennis-balls and so on.

No. 4 brought the flag but no stick, so it was draped somewhat loosely on the top, where it remained for about two months.

Here it should be recorded that, about twelve feet from the top, a wedge of stone weighing about ten pounds detached itself from the upper surface of one of the stone knobs. Just here the turret is vertical, and though the knobs seemed safe the climber was fortunately climbing correctly, not moving a hand or foot until the other three holds were secured. As his right hand-hold fell away he instinctively looked down to watch the stone fall. In the darkness he could not see it, but as it broke into fragments on the roof over fifty feet below the sound brought a shudder to his companion.

Examination of the mementoes the next morning brought to light the interesting fact that the tops of the knobs were covered with green lichen. As the climber was wearing gym shoes, and odd spots of rain were falling at the time of the climb, he must have come near to having a very slippery time.

Cronies were pulled from their beds and made to celebrate with the happy climbers. Bill, returning to Pembroke from Caius at 3.30 a.m., put his head in at the window to see what was happening, and joined the party.

Then comes one of those sly touches of humour which are too perfect for comment. The authorities (towards whom we have developed very tender feelings) faced the matter squarely and set their steeplejacks to work. They did not alter the lock of the spiral staircase; they did not affix a burglar alarm to the base of the spires. Arguing that since climbers could get up without it the conductor did not matter, and they put it back in the chimney.

Soon after this a number of men were planning to enlist in the service of the Ethiopian Emperor. Charles of Pembroke was one, and there were three army officers and an army sergeant. The scheme did not materialize for two reasons. First, the officers found that they could not resign their commissions in time, as they thought, to get out before the railway was cut. It would have taken nearly three months, when they felt it would be too late. Secondly, an untimely bump on the head brought Charles's career to a close. It was an interesting scheme, and was very far developed before it was finally abandoned.

This wild scheme in which Charles was involved may have been part of the cause of the next climb, on April 26th, 1936. Charles was dead, and he had dearly wanted to climb the Chapel. Why not climb it for him, and at the same time strike a blow for the cause he had wanted to champion? A friend of Charles organized the "Save Ethiopia" plot.

One of the officers who had visited the Ethiopian Imperial Lega-tion several times offered to obtain help from the Legation. A word to the wise is sufficient, and he returned from the interview with a mag-nificent specimen of the Ethiopian tri-colour twelve feet by six. This was attached to an eight-foot pole. A Union Jack was also bought.

Charles's Cambridge friend then bought a piece of white linen, thirteen yards long by forty-two inches deep. The lady in the shop quite believed him when he said he was going to make a kilt. He bought three pots of "Jet-Glaze", and with a friend painted the words "Save Ethiopia". They sewed sticks into the ends, wherewith to provide a good hold for the ropes.

Then they went up on to the roof, two climbers and two onlookers, using the precious key. Carrying a hundred-foot rope, a forty-foot knotted rope, two miniature flag-poles and a rolled-up streamer, they felt pleasantly encumbered.

Each taking a turret, the climbers reached the top, and lowered a string for the flags. No. 2 rapidly affixed his flag and descended to the parapet. Here he fumed and wondered what in the name of fortune had possessed No. 1.

For No. 1 was in a quandary. He had lost the two bits of string wherewith to tie the flag to the point of the lightning-conductor, and had to hold the flag while he chewed off two more bits of string – a lengthy and tiring business. He longed for the canine incisors of his simian ancestors, and replied to the testy enquiries of No. 2 that he was "looking at the view".

These climbers were utterly indifferent to the noise they made.

At length he was ready, and descended to the parapet. The streamer was hauled up on each side. Visions of a conscience-stricken Cambridge waking up in the morning to send donations to the Ethiopian Imperial Legation rose in the minds of all concerned. It was not to be, however.

All the witches in *Macbeth* seemed to have lent their winds for the purpose of blowing down the streamer. The tremendous flappings began to cause uneasiness even among the noise-immune quartet. Then, on the north-east turret, it tore away from the fastening rope, right across the forty-two inches of fabric.

The next minute was rather more unpleasant than the turn at the circus when a man in velveteens cracks a long whip. Swinging out horizontally over the grass by King's Parade, it made a noise which could have been heard half a mile away. The climbers were now in a serious state of alarm. There was a considerable likelihood that the whip-cracks of the streamer would awaken the porter in his lodge a hundred yards away. The policeman on his short beat was bound to hear it, wherever he was. In quick time No. 2 hauled in the noisy tongue of propaganda.

Nobody seemed to have heard. The streamer was hung out of the wind, below roof level. Here it was taken down by the porters before nine o'clock.

To prevent this, or rather to enable the press to obtain a photograph, the climbers rang up two newspapers in London, waking up the sleepy operator from a telephone-box. Although the press tried to obtain the names of the climbers, they maintained their modest anonymity, for which they were later to thank their lucky stars.

When the calls were over, the operator rang up the college, repeated what he had heard and apologized for not having obtained the names of the climbers. So does prudence occasionally rear up its head in triumph.

It was prudence, too, which caused three of the climbers to prevent the fourth from executing his idea of the Dean's Umbrella. This idea, which occurred to him on the roof, was to seal the turret door for an hour or two to delay the porters until the press photographers had obtained a picture of the streamer.

The turret door opens inwards into a passage about three feet wide. The climber – it was the butterfly-collector – wanted to lay an umbrella across the passage as they were closing the door, so as to seal the turret. A message to the head porter would later have explained that the door could be opened with a determined push, which would have the effect of breaking the dean's umbrella. However, there was a danger that the umbrella would be stubborn and refuse to break, and the possibility of the porters having to smash open the door or put scaffolding up to the roof caused the idea to be abandoned.

It would perhaps scarcely be a digression to include the tale of the travelling steeplejacks, since it concerns the removal of the flags.

The president of the C.U. Mountaineering Club, a Kingsman, offered to go up and take down the flags for the authorities. This was mentioned at a special college meeting, and it was arranged that he should go up after lunch. A junior don was to direct the climb and the chaplain was to take photographs. While this was being discussed, some steeplejacks who had been working on Ely Cathedral drove into Cambridge.

They took their chance. Ringing up the college, they offered to take down the flag. The dean or bursar, not certain that a mere mountaineer could be trusted on the Chapel, rapidly clinched the deal with them and told them to waste no time. By midday their task was over and the ladders were being removed.

The college authorities were grievously shocked at the idea of the red, yellow and green of Ethiopia adorning a prominent building. For this reason, the two climbers lay very low. The names of their assistants became known (among the *Élite*) but for months scarcely a soul in Cambridge knew the principals. So far as we know, this is the first time that the full story has been published. The dean paid his cheque of twenty pounds to the steeplejacks, and wise heads met once more in consultation.

They decided that the climbers had used the spiral staircase, as the conductor had obviously not been touched. So they put a Yale lock on the door, whose key could not be duplicated, making George's key an interesting relic. No more should the staircase be used.

The torch now passed to Nazareth College. A tall fourth-year man had for three years coveted the letters C.C. (Chapel Climber) after his name. He chose this moment to earn them.

Traverse round base of pinnacle. There is a drop of 100ft below the climber.

Assuming the "Save Ethiopia" party to have gone up the outside, he went along to the chimney in the north-east corner one night soon after twelve. With him he had a penknife, and with this he prised the flat ribbon conductor away from the wall until he could get his fingers behind.

Unused to chimneying, and having to pull the conductor away at every step, he found it very tiring. He records that he found it a "rather frightening business", and did not realize his height until with a shock he found he could see over the roof of the Old Library. Once on the roof he rested for three-quarters of an hour; the whole climb took him two and a half hours. He had ricked his back on the way up. Using the conductor to yank himself over the two overhangs, he affixed a swastika to the pinnacle.

No mountaineer, he had previously done a considerable amount of roof-rambling, but no serious roof-climbing. He simply achieved it alone, without previous preparation or training, as a sheer *tour de force*. He tells us that on reaching the back gate he was too exhausted to climb out and had to lie down for a further half-hour. And yet, when in a similar state on the roof of the Chapel, he had managed to force himself to go on and complete the climb. For stark valour this takes some beating.

And so, in spite of the new key, the dean had to pay out another twenty pounds. Quite apart from any personal disapproval, one can understand him feeling somewhat annoyed.

Lastly, we come to the blunderings of our own party.

In the effort to get good photographs our own party has been on the Chapel on five occasions. Starting in midsummer, and continuing in the dead of winter when Cambridge shivered under its congealed eiderdown, there were only two occasions worth recording. First to be told is how two members of the party were caught on the Chapel.

There were four in the party; two climbers, a camera-man and a flashlight-man. There was some scaffolding from the ground to the roof in the south-west corner, of which the party availed itself, as only the pinnacles were to be photographed that night. The original idea was for a climber and the flash-man to install themselves on the parapet of the south-east pinnacle, to photograph the other climber on the north-east pinnacle, fifty or more feet away. However, to haul a man weighing nearly fourteen stone up forty feet to the parapet was more than the climbers could manage. Also, he hoped to get a rowing blue, and had had orders from the president of the C.U.B.C. to do no climbing with us. (The whole boat-club received this order, which deprived us of three of our best climbers.)

So the arrangement was slightly altered, and with a camera on the parapet and the flash on the roof, the other climber went up the north-east spire. He was about fifteen feet from the top when he saw a policeman walk up to the Porters' Lodge. He heard the bell ring twice, and in a minute two lights went on. The porters were dressing.

It seemed too late to consider escaping, so the climber did not worry the others with what he had seen. If you must be caught he argued, get the photograph first.

With typical cussedness, the reflector now refused to work. They banged it, they shook and rattled it, cajoled it in every way they could, but it would not work. Bellows of advice echoed from pinnacle to parapet and from parapet to roof-level, with answers coming from the roof equally loudly. The lights went out in the Porters' Lodge; the Chapel was surrounded.

After the apparatus had been taken to pieces and put together again, a couple of flashes were finally extorted from it. By this time the

Standing on the first overhang.

climbers had been in their respective stations for half an hour. There was a cold east wind blowing (the date was December 16th) and the wait became a matter of endurance. Extremely lightly clad as they both were to ensure facility of movement, the man on the pinnacle wore only four articles of clothing. His bare feet were as cold as the stone on which they stood; his fingers were also numb, and he tried in vain to warm them under this armpits. The other climber was in an equally dire state. With extremities devoid of feeling, the descent from the top was difficult.

On the roof the situation was explained and discussed. Two of the party were King's undergraduates, which made it all the more problematical. At all costs these two must escape.

The scaffolding was in the south-west corner. There was a hope, meagre though it was, that the porters would concentrate at the foot of this scaffolding and not watch the chimney in the north-east corner. The climbers offered to lower the others down this on the rope and then follow themselves. They shone a torch down and explained the science of chimneying. The other two were manfully gulping down their terror when a torch shone from below and a voice called up:

"Come down, Mr H., come down."

They had recognized the voice of the butterfly-collector of 1934.

He replied in an amiable tone that he would go down the scaffolding, and the situation was rapidly discussed. It was decided that the two Kingsmen should stay on the roof, and the other two go down. They were marched off to the Porters' Lodge to await the arrival of the Senior Dean.

In pyjamas and mortar-board he duly arrived, and a discussion took place between three policemen, two porters, two deans and two delinquents. In the soul-shattering stress of the moment, the flash-man started talking broad Scotch without being aware of the fact; he had spent the first six years of his life in Scotland.

Remembering a statement he had once heard that it is impossible to argue against an assumption, the butterfly-collector treated the affair as unfortunate but laughable. With blood oozing from every finger he opened the suitcase and showed the bulbs, explaining also how to work the reflector. He showed the camera, and talked of apertures and focusing, and how difficult it was to point the camera correctly in the dark. He spoke as though he were revealing secrets that he would only tell to a friend. As the junior dean remarked to a colleague the next day: "They were so polite and confidential that it was impossible to speak severely to them".

Next came the Pigou argument. We mention this because Kingsmen at least attach importance to it, poppycock though it is, and it may have deterred several men from attempting the Chapel. It is always delivered in the same form. "Professor Pigou says the stonework on the Chapel is not safe." It is a very effective argument.

The climber agreed that Pigou was a potent name, but suggested that his own experience differed from that of the professor. But the dean then reminded the climber of a piece of stone he had dislodged when coming down, and which had provided the porters below with a major thrill.

This was a trivial point, but it made argument difficult.

Although the climber did not mention the fact, it was not stone, but a staple of the conductor which he had dislodged. Slightly anxious about the numbness of his fingers, he had followed the line of the conductor, gripping it at intervals with a necessarily clumsy grasp. It was this clumsy grasp that had dislodged the staple.

The flash-man was made to promise to destroy the photographs in the camera. This he reluctantly promised to do, though later his reluctance changed to a chortle. The photographer had pointed wrongly, and all he had promised to destroy was a couple of photographs of the black wall of heaven.

Finally, the senior dean told them to return to Bedford. Fortunately it had occurred to no one that the flash-man might be an undergraduate, and all was well. After having had three-quarters of an hour's talk, they went for a couple of hours' sleep on the floor of a room in Pembroke Street before going to Bedford, leaving the lodge at seven minutes past five.

At ten minutes past five the two Kingsmen, stealing across the college, came to the safety of their own rooms. Theirs had been an interesting escape.

When the scapegoats had gone down the scaffolding it seemed certain that the porters would go up to the roof, and something had to be done. Eric tried the turret door, and found that for once it was not bolted. After going through, he bolted it from the inside, a very wise precaution.

He found that the wire door above was not shut, and they went up, so as not to meet any porters who might come up the spiral staircase. After ten minutes they went down, expecting to find the door locked. So it was, but they opened it and went into the Chapel, where they sat for half an hour in the Provost's pew. They then left by the north-west door, which they locked behind them. They skulked along close to Clare, and so got along by a wide detour to their rooms. This was fortunate, as they would otherwise have met the two deans returning from the lodge.

Thus they left no trace there they had been, except possibly a dent in the Provost's cushion. Having come through three doors, they left every door locked or bolted behind them. There was no magic in it; they knew where to find the keys.

The interest of this escape lies in the fact that it was practically proof against all possibilities. Recording the incident at length in the log-book, Eric says: "I am in fact beginning to doubt whether we were really there at all! There is little more... We retired to bed at 6 a.m. Since when we have had the constant pleasure of listening to the deans relating at length, to an admiring audience, how the efficient college organization deals with would-be Chapel climbers!"

This man we call Eric, a quietly self-sufficient soul, has for long been a special favourite of the senior dean, just as the butterfly-collector considers himself his pet aversion. When not in bad company Eric is astonishingly virtuous. The coolness with which he sometimes substitutes crime for good behaviour is only equalled by the infectious efficiency which he has brought to bear on our problems. We feel especially proud of him, in that we chose him on character alone, asking him to join us first from the host of non-climbing acquaintances who might have been asked. After a few outings he proved to be a brilliant climber; the best photographs in this book were taken by him, and in other ways he has proved invaluable. Quiet as he is and with few friends, strangers usually assume that he is going into holy orders. He would make a good parson, though he undoubtedly suffers from kleptomania. His avoidance of superlatives in speech is only equalled by his attainment of them in action.

The other climb that we mentioned is worth recording because it took place in daylight. Attempts to take flashlight photographs of the chimney from above had been completely unsuccessful, and it was felt that it would be difficult to sight the camera efficiently in the dark while leaning over the edge. The alternative that remained was to do it in daylight.

The idea occurred to two climbers as they were lunching together one day. There were workmen on the south side of the building, so that the climb must be done in the lunch hour.

It was already well after half-past one when they started. One, an undergraduate from Trinity, obtained the key to the turret from the Chapel clerk. He could thus claim detachment if trouble should arise. When he was ready the other started; he came up more slowly than he had previously done, and arrived fresh at the top. After a few minutes' chat he went up to the parapet of the north-east spire. Here he felt horribly exposed to view and abandoned his idea of going to the top. He could see dozens of people in the street, and several in the college. In particular, he could see the bulky form of the junior dean walking round the college, having only to look up to see him. As the climber was once more the butterfly-collector who had recently been caught, his reluctance to go to the top may be pardoned.

Back on roof-level he stopped to talk for two or three minutes before going down. On the ground he looked at his watch. He had been twenty-seven minutes. As he had climbed all but the last thirty feet and had taken the climb very easily, it would seem that the complete climb could be accomplished in half an hour. This actual climber is of the opinion that he could do it in twenty minutes, but this is doubtful. He spent ten minutes in the chimney; six going up and four going down. Within half an hour of leaving the Chapel they were on the roof of Trinity Library, whence they had the interesting escape mentioned in a previous chapter.

The latest from the Chapel front is that at the moment of writing the authorities are planning some new abomination to make the Chapel more difficult. What counter-move have they decided upon? Are they going to put revolving spikes in the four corner chimneys? Patient generations of climbers will remove them with steel files. Are they going to put bird-lime on the overhangs, to suspend climbers from their hands while their feet hang in space? The counter-movers will surmount it on stilts, or drop on to the pinnacle with a parachute. Are they going to attach a burglar-alarm to the lightning-conductor? Practical jokers will wake up the porters in the night watches with playful nips at the alarm.

We once heard someone express the entrancing theory that the night climbers are subsidized by the Steeplejacks' Union. This idea, though probably as gross an exaggeration as the report of Mark Twain's death, offers up some intriguing possibilities to the mercenary minded.

And so the tradition of the Chapel goes on. Each individual climber continues his separate career, becoming a polar explorer, a don, or collecting butterflies. Among past Chapel climbers we know of three polar explorers, seven dons or schoolmasters, and at least two who collect butterflies. Sometimes those experiences crowd back upon the memory, and the past flashes back like a distant peak momentarily lighted up by a sunbeam piercing through the clouds. Then oblivion again. Strange it is how the prosaic present may hide the exciting past.

But the Chapel, that will never be prosaic. Those who have seen it outlined against the sunset or the full moon, those who have seen its sloping leaded roof-top glisten after a shower of rain, those who have looked down upon the world from its summit, all those who have seen these things will remember the poetry that it has taught them. And while each man changes from year to year, going through the continual changes that make a lifetime, the Chapel remains always the same. When the rest of Cambridge is crumbling and in ruins, the Chapel will still be standing, the last to fall to time as it is the last to fall to climbers.

CHAPTER FOURTEEN

The Chapel Again

*"Follow my heels, Rugby"**

Merry Wives

NOW FOR a detailed description of the climb. It falls into two natural stages, ground to roof, and roof to pinnacle. Each stage is severe. Ground to roof without the lightning-conductor falls into the select aristocracy of climbs, the very severe type. All the same it is quite feasible.

The first thing, if you are not a Kingsman, is to climb into college. This is easy. The writer has used nine different ways, without using the simplest method of all, that of punting down from Silver Street. About half a dozen ways are equally easy, and the roof-climbing connoisseur will be able, if he has nothing better to do, to count up to forty or fifty possible ways.

But the reader is advised not to follow the lead of one drunken Kingsman, who in full evening dress entered via the coal-hole. As his bed-maker said to him the next morning, "You didn't ought to do it".

There is no night porter wandering about in King's. The authorities

---

* At the moment of writing the last three Chapel climbers have been Old Rugbeians.

Chimney from below.

pay you the compliment, ugly gate-crasher, of treating you as a grown-up. And since we are not grown-up, you and I, we will perform our midnight frolics as the inmates burn the midnight oil. Give them their due. It is past one o'clock, and a number of lights are still burning, sign that bulging brains are cramming themselves to bursting point. Kingsmen work hard, and as a result the authorities trust them more than the undergraduates of any other college. And to be serious for a moment, there is more friendship and understanding between dons and undergraduates in this college than in any other.

Now concentrate. We are in college, padding over grass by the side of the gravel paths to reach the Chapel. If seen by anyone, draw your gown round your chin, mutter Latin and look ghoulish, furtive, Rabelaisian, or what you will. The passer-by will then take no notice.

And when the Chapel looms close you may perhaps remember the words of Browning quoted by the *Guide to Trinity*:

Though there's doorway behind thee and window before,
Go straight at the wall.

As the walls rise up above you, dark and forbidding, your heart flings itself against the four walls of its prison, as though sensing a pall in the blackness of the shadows above.

We reach the Chapel without incident. If it is before midnight, the lamp-post opposite the main door will cause us to walk warily. After midnight, all is quiet and serenity. We may pass a don or a couple of undergraduates taking a breath of fresh air before turning in to bed, but that is all.

The four corner turrets each have a chimney, but one is outstandingly the best both for climbing and seclusion. This is the chimney on

Two-thirds of the way up.

the north-east turret, at the end of the north wall, as distinguished from the chimney at the other side of the turret, in K.P. It is in college, the revolving spikes over the railings being only a few feet away. None save the moon and the winking stars is likely to see you, though you might be detected from the windows of Clare. Immediately opposite is the Old Library, a building virtually uninhabited by night. There are some bushes about, and a wooden hut with a corrugated iron roof. A steel-pointed arrow, falling on to this roof from a dizzy height in the sky, once caused a serious fright to four Chapel climbers.

This is where you draw a deep breath and begin.

If we are taking up some heavy or inconvenient impedimenta with us, it may be wise for one man to go up first with a ball of string in his pocket. He can then lower it, and haul up the luggage before No. 2 climbs up. Or, if there be an accomplice on the ground, we can both climb up together.

It is not wise for more than two of us to climb at once. The top man may find the conductor pulled by the other two so close to the wall through the clamps that it is almost useless to him. Even with two of us this is inclined to happen. It is safer to go up singly.

As you go into the corner, you find horizontal bands of stone which make it easy to ascend the first four feet. You find the conductor, running down the wall from clamp to clamp like a series of elongated D's (see photograph). It is just over an inch wide, and about a fifth of an inch deep. It will probably make the palms of your hands slightly sore.

On this, the first pitch, the breadth of the chimney scarcely exceeds the length of a man's thigh. Only a Tom Thumb could hope to manoeuvre upwards without the conductor. A tall man must pull himself up almost entirely with his arms. Of the whole climb, this pitch

Nearing the top.

of fifteen or twenty feet is the most severe on the arms, and tends to tire them at the outset.

Soon, however, there comes a broad, sloping ledge where you may sit and rest as long as you wish. Then the chimney proper begins.

As may be seen from the photographs, it is of an ideal width for a climber. There is nothing to prevent him from mounting upwards at a rapid rate, and the conductor will prevent him from slipping sideways. It should be used for balance alone, as it is quite easy to climb with the legs. The stone flange against which the feet are pressed is about four inches wide, and as the side wall is at right angles to the main wall, the climber must be at a slightly oblique angle. It proceeds like this for about sixty feet and then, for the last ten feet, becomes a few inches wider.

This chimney, though considered formidable on account of its length (the roof is ninety feet from the ground), is so straightforward that one is tempted to wonder whether it could be done without the lightning-conductor. We mentioned the case of the don who is supposed to have got up without using it, but having it close at hand must have been a great comfort. A don in Trinity tells us that he got up half-way without using it, but had to lay a hand on it coming down. We have called the chimney severe, but this is more owing to its psychological effect than to any technical difficulty. Anyone who has once done it would do it again, rain or fine, tired or fresh, drunk or sober, and think nothing of it. A really severe climb, however often one does it, still commands the respect of the climber.

Of course, the twenty feet up to the first ledge would be unclimb-able, but there are loose ladders about in the college which should overcome the first pitch. Professor Pigou, whom we have already referred to in the last chapter, is also sometimes quoted as saying: "With the conductor, any fool could climb up to the roof. Without it,

King's Chapel, North-East Pinnacle. Negotiating the first overhang. Note bare feet. The climber's back is dirty through having just come up the main chimney from the ground.

only a fool would do so." We agree with him. All climbers who have climbed the chimney and to whom we have spoken think that without the conductor it would still be possible.

It is possible, but it requires intense concentration. The body has an unpleasant tendency to slip away to the left, and the more oblique it is, the harder it is to get back. Without the conductor, the climber must go very slowly, and maintain complete control over body and mind during every fraction of a second of the climb. During the two years that it was without a conductor, the chimney was not climbed, but this was probably because the vast majority of undergraduates did not know it was possible. If ever the authorities remove the conductor again, we are confident that the Chapel will nevertheless be climbed.

But having got up, the climber must get down again. Without a rope or conductor this would be very severe, for descending a chimney is considerably harder than ascending. At the best, he would be taking a heavy risk, and no climber should do this. It would be possible to climb without the conductor and yet take no risks, but not to descend. So there must be a rope.

This is where we remember the butterfly collector of 1934. The rope must be hanging from directly above the chimney. And we don't want to provide the authorities with another bell-rope. So get two hundred-foot ropes, and tie them together.

Now pass the rope over the parapet above the chimney, with one length in the chimney. Pass the other end round the turret to an accomplice on the grass by King's Parade. The friction will be such that he can hold it easily with one hand, and the party can descend in safety.

For such a climb without the conductor, the leader must be a tall man, as the short-legged climber might find the last ten feet somewhat too broad. But at the moment of writing the conductor makes it easy.

Chapel Spire. A: First overhang, with clover leaf above and below.
B: second overhang, with parapet just above.
C: Chess-board, at which point the stone becomes crumbly.
With three simultaneous grips for the rest of the way up the climb is safe.

Enough of the chimney.

We are now on the roof, and from here the turrets do not look very formidable.

Mounting on the stone balustrade of the roof, we can step on to the sloping slab of stone a few feet up the turret. In front of us are air-holes for the hollow turret, each hole shaped rather like a clover-leaf. The holes are about fifteen inches deep and across, and are situated one above the other in a single row. The turret is octagonal, and on each side of us is an ornamental corner pillar. We call them ornamental because they support no weight, but they are quite smooth. No fancy flower designs festoon them.

The pillars are about four feet to four feet six inches apart. The climber may be tempted to chimney between them, but finds it is just impossible.

To begin with, however, he can use the clover-leaf air-holes as a ladder. There is wire behind them to keep out the pigeons, but with care you can get your fingers through the wire. After a few feet you come to the first overhang.

The pillars stand out vertically, away from the face. The overhang consists of a V-shaped projection reaching out as far as the pillar, and then sloping back again. For five feet there is no hand-hold. The tip of the V, it is true, is flat for about nine inches, but it is then rounded, and so is useless save as a pressure-hold, pressing downwards. It is best to ignore this ledge until you can get a knee or foot on to it.

With the overhang above you, hold the clover-leaf with your left hand. Pass your right arm affectionately round the pillar. The square angle on the far side provides a friction finger-grip which prevents you from falling outwards.

Double one foot under you in the chimneying position. You now find that the inner side of the pillar, being square cut, faces the clover-leaf up which you have been climbing. You can now chimney and wriggle upwards.

Above the clover-leaf hole is an ornamental hollow, useless as a hand-hold, but excellent for the feet. You get a foot into this, and are thus standing above the last hand-hold.

The middle of the overhang should now be level with your waist. By leaning forward (still keeping your right arm round the pillar) you can reach the clover-leaf above the overhang. In your hurry don't get your little finger pinched between the wire and the stone, and don't hold the wire alone. Get your fingers through it on to the stone, so that you need not depend upon the security of the wire. You can now get a knee on to the ledge of the overhang, and your first difficulty is over.

There next comes ten feet of clover-leaf ladder, and you are up against the second overhang.

If you are a purist, you will find it more difficult than the first, though the principle is the same. But most climbers probably choose the face where there is a drain-pipe.

This pipe is of no help on any of the turrets, except at the top. Very conveniently, it ends three feet from the parapet, half-way up the overhang. It ends in an open bowl, and is firmly clamped to the wall. You can grasp this bowl without chimneying. It is a foot or eighteen inches behind you.

Leaning boldly outwards and grasping the bowl with both hands, you can walk up the clover-leaf with your feet up to the top-most hole. With your head level with the drain-pipe bowl you can grasp the battle-mented parapet, and in a moment you are up, using the bowl as your last foot-hold. The stone-work of the parapet is perfectly firm.

You are now on the parapet, forty feet above roof level.

Here we will leave you for a moment, and go down again to roof-level.

In the last chapter we said there were two alternative methods of surmounting the overhangs (or with the drain-pipe, three for the second). The second method is more obvious and easier, but requires a steady head.

We get on to the slabs, ten feet above roof-level. Standing very upright, we pass an arm round the pillar. The other hand holds the near-side edge of the pillar. As the two inside edges point inwards, they provide ample friction-hold against falling outwards. We now pass our body very gingerly round the pillar. Then upwards and forwards, up to the clover-leaf. Then round the next pillar, and so on until we reach the lightning-conductor, by whose help we can easily surmount the overhangs and rejoin you on the parapet.

So next time, you can take your choice. If you go round to the conductor, you will make one of the most sensational traverses in climbing. As you pass round each pillar, the whole of your body except your hands and feet are over black emptiness. Your feet are on slabs of stone sloping downwards and outwards at an angle of about thirty-five degrees to the horizontal, your fingers and elbows making the most of a friction-hold against a vertical pillar, and the ground is precisely one hundred feet directly below you. If you slip, you will still have three seconds to live.

However, if it has not rained for twelve hours, this hyper-sensational traverse is not difficult.

As you step on to the parapet, a flurry of pigeons may disturb you. Numbers of them sleep inside the parapet. You even may, as has been done before, put your foot actually on to a bird. The surprise will be mutual, but don't step back and raise your hands in Victorian fashion.

And be assured, though the flapping of the birds is tremendous, no one on the ground seems to notice it.

The turret has now become somewhat smaller in girth. There is more clover-leaf for about eight feet, but this time it is free of wire mesh, so that you can put your hands through and obtain really good holds.

At the top of this comes your last difficulty, requiring careful rather than unduly skilled climbing.

The clover-leaf stops, and a four-inch ledge is about two feet above it. This is not very satisfactory, as there is no finger-grip, and one must counter the tendency to fall outwards.

However, looking down, you will see the corner pillar projecting about five feet above the parapet, tapering up to a point about as big as your fist. You can stand on this with one foot, and by putting most of your weight upon it, will evade the outward tendency. This one small foot-hold, appearing in space out of the darkness, has something weird about it. It gives you a peculiar sensation, and you feel like an ant balancing on a needle. The projection of the pillar is quite safe, as it is secured to the turret by an iron bar.

Now, to negotiate the next few feet. On the left, at arm's length, is an ornamentation known as the chess-board. In size and shape it is akin to a square block of electric light bulbs. On no account use this. The bulb-shaped projections of the stone form tempting hand-holds, and are probably safe. But they are not very big, and should one break off you will not be able to recover yourself.

On the right, at about the same level, is the first gargoyle,* sticking out horizontally for fifteen or eighteen inches. You will have to use it and at one moment to put a considerable amount of weight

---

* We call them gargoyles, because that is what they most resemble. Strictly speaking, however, they are not gargoyles but plain blocks of stone.

The last thirty feet.

Notice by the Vice-Chancellor

TWO PERSONS *in statu pupillari*, having been found climbing King's College Chapel, have been rusticated by their Colleges.

G. H. A. WILSON,
Vice-Chancellor.

10 June 1937

upon it. This, if you have read the previous chapter, is where you will remember the story about the sliver of stone which came off the upper surface of a gargoyle. You put your hand upon it, and the moment is fraught with care.

The gargoyle is slightly thicker than a man's thigh, and you can get no finger-grip. To avoid all danger, press downwards upon it, rather than downwards and sideways. The surface cannot then crumble off. You may perhaps find it convenient to get both hands round it, with the fingers locked. You will then be able to walk up to the top clover-leaf, and reach out to the gargoyle on the left.

From now on the climb is easy. You are entering upon the bottle-neck, which is about seventy to seventy-five degrees to the horizontal, but after the unrelieved vertical ascent feels like crawling on one's belly over flat ground. Numerous gargoyles seem to appear everywhere, like the arms of an old yew tree. In a few moments we are at the top.

Standing on two of the three spacious pseudo-gargoyles four feet from the top, you can clasp your hands round the stone, the top of which is level with your chest. The lightning-conductor, a friendly and inflexible steel rod as thick as your finger (very different from that in the chimney), sticks up for another three feet. The top has a circlet of three firm spikes, so that if you wish you can stand on the tippety top of the stone. We do not advise this, as in such airy places the wind is fitful and uncertain, and a gust may come out of a calm night.

What do you feel as you are standing at the top? Triumph? Awe? A sense of great height? Fear? Anxiety about the descent?

Perhaps the first feeling is one of disappointment. The ambition of which you have been dreaming for weeks, or even months, is finished, and you must find another to replace it. You have been dreaming, glorying in the thought of it, and now in a few drab moments after the thrill of endeavour you are in the throes of success. You are standing on the peak of what is held to be a considerable achievement. Climbers may think that unknown heroes have been at work, and only you know yourself for what you are, a very naked body behind it all. You feel a usurper, a filcher of honours which the truly brave would scorn to earn. The height does not inspire you. You simply feel a very insignificant man standing on a monument of insignificance.

But the exaltation will come later. When all is over, you will enjoy facing your bed-maker's cross-examination, replying to her queries by a bland look of innocence and a rather fatuous grin. You will bounce about with tremendous satisfaction, and feel more pleasure in living than you have ever known. The exaltation resulting from a difficult climb lasts for about three days, and during this time you will feel the devil of a fellow.

CHAPTER FIFTEEN

Saying Good-bye

"I am going, O Nokomis,
On a long and distant journey
But these guests I leave behind me,
In your watch and ward I leave them;
See that never harm comes near them,
See that never fear molests them,
Never danger nor suspicion,
Never want of food or shelter,
In the lodge of Hiawatha!"

Hiawatha

ALL THAT now remains is to take our leave, as gracefully as may be, and melt away into the darkness we have loved. The narrow line which separates the sublime from the ludicrous runs through time as well as space, and we have reached that line. No longer may we test ourselves up pipe and chimney; the days of early manhood become as out of date as those of the nursery, and we must say farewell.

There is a French saying that the first love is the only true one. Probably this is more true of places than of people. Somewhere in the heart of every one of us there is a place he loves more than anywhere else. It may be his old school, or the place where he was born; his present home, or somewhere where he spent a holiday with particularly vivid associations. He might be able to give no valid reason for his preference, but it is there, and time, which dims other memories, keeps these fresh. Across the choppy tide of time certain landmarks stand out, motionless and fixed in the receding waters. Some of them we can talk about, some we keep very secret, but we all have them. They are the unseen milestones of our journey, unseen often to ourselves until a certain light reveals them for a few moments, like the sun casting a silhouette of distant islands. Or perhaps there is but one, marking a corner which none but ourselves know we have turned.

Whatever it is, we each have something like this on which to look back. And thinking about it, we realize that love is infectious, and spreads of its own accord. We may love a place where we loved a person, or a person whom we met in a place we loved. Things interconnect strangely with unforeseen results coming from simple events, and from a simple love, if it be intense enough, the focus may blur and the light increase, until we find ourselves possessed of an overwhelming love of everything around us.

We ourselves have loved Cambridge. Many hundreds of young men must go through the same experience every year, for the undergraduate is at an emotionally susceptible age. To each it comes in its own way, each accepts it according to his character. Memories of Cambridge may conjure up old friends, weeks and months of hard work followed by successful exams, thrills on the football field, morning coffee in the cafes, convivial evenings of beer-drinking, hilarious twenty-first birthday parties. But not to us. Cambridge brings back a jumble of pipes and chimneys and pinnacles, leading up from security to adventure.

We think of those nights spent with one or more friends, nights when we merged with the shadows and could see the world with eyes that were not our own.

Now it is all over, and as the evening draws on we sit in an armchair by the fireside, comfortable with slippers and a book. When the hour comes that we should go out, in a polo sweater and black gym shoes, we yawn and think of bed. We resist the temptation to steal another hour from the night, to read another chapter. There are new worlds to conquer, and we must be ready.

The future is waiting, in its smile a tremendous invitation, and we must try to win favours from it. It will not tolerate half-heartedness, and as it absorbs our energies we think less and less of those great moments of the past. Already, we seldom live through them again. Yet since this is a farewell, and we are stepping out of yesterday into tomorrow, we will lay down the book and answer questions we have never before asked ourselves.

First, why did we start night climbing? Was it an irrepressible gambling instinct, with ourselves the dice, and the pleasure of teasing destiny as our winnings? Was it an attempt to emulate men we knew to be better than ourselves, and by doing what they did to imagine ourselves their equals? Was it the hypnotism of an immense terror drawing us in in spite of ourselves? Was it sheer animal spirits finding an outlet?

Certainly not the latter. All the former reasons may have played their part, for human motives are more complex than the strangest chemical compound. The primary cause was probably an urgent need for self-discipline, though this quickly gave way to enjoyment of the thrills that came. Chance also played its part.

One autumn day some years ago we were slowly walking through Cambridge, in despair at our utter inefficiency. There was no taste in anything. Nothing was so easy but was too difficult, the lightest task was too much effort. We had just missed a supervision because it had seemed too much trouble to walk across the court. Life had sunk to a stage of sitting vacantly and waiting for the next meal. A complete and permanent lack of interest had set in. Something drastic was needed.

Summoning the last vestiges of mental energy, we vowed to do the hardest thing we could think of. Instead of failing, through lack of interest, in the multitude of things that had grown so tiresome, we would come back to life, not quietly, but with a gigantic achievement as a kick-off. It was the only hope. With something like this behind us, the effort of living would become easier, and the successful effort would embody itself in our character. But what was there that we could possibly find to serve the purpose? It was the darkest hour.

At this moment we looked up and saw the spires of King's Chapel. Here was the answer. Though we had known the fascination, we had always felt a strong fear of heights. We had no qualifications, mental or physical, for the job, except a strong desire not to jellify into permanent unconsciousness. If we could do it, we should recover. Thus we started night climbing.

Many climbers probably start somewhat in the same way. It is one of the simplest ways in which a man can come to grips with the deficiencies of his character. He may be full of fears; in climbing he can conquer them and see himself doing it. From the height he reaches, his range of vision increases, and he sees himself as well as the world around him. Imagination is brought into play. A mere cog, he finds himself in sympathy with the machine. Climbing can bring only good to those who indulge in it; it is a stimulus from which there is no reaction.

If we are so often frightened while climbing, why do we enjoy it? This is a harder question to answer. It is partly the sense of achievement, partly the thrill of taking apparently big risks when subconsciously we know the danger to be very small. "If this or that should happen," a climber is continually telling himself, "I shall go spinning." Yet he knows it will not happen. A hand-hold may occasionally break off, but never the vital one he is forced to trust. The sense of danger is much greater than the danger itself.

It is probably the sense of danger which is the basis of the stimulus which comes from climbing. Fear, in its cruder forms, is protective. The nearness of the danger increases the sensibility of the mind, puts keenness on to the mental edge. A climber is enlivened by an appeal to the same instincts which came into the daily life of his ancestors. Nothing is so precious as when we seem to have run a risk of losing it.

For a climber is a man standing on the edge of an abyss. The chance of falling over or of the ground crumbling beneath his feet is negligible, yet his very closeness to the edge makes him think. He cannot but visualize what would happen if he stepped forward, and realizes with a shock of what very small significance it would be. The sun would still be shining, and the waterfall would still be roaring below. And suddenly he realizes, perhaps for the first time in his life, what a friendly fellow the sun is, what vividness there is in the green around him.

There is a kind of fear which is very closely akin to love, and this is the fear which the climber enjoys. It is, to use a contradictory term, a brave fear; a fear which announces its presence, perhaps very loudly, but raises no insuperable barrier to achievement. The climber enjoys being frightened, because he knows the fear is no impediment.

Lastly, we may ask ourselves whether the good effects resulting from climbing are permanent. From the pinnacle of our premature old age, we think we can say they are.

Flashlight, bulbs, rucksack, camera, ropes and men.

The immediate exaltation after a difficult climb only lasts two or three days at the outside, but there is a residual effect after the effervescence has died down. The imagination, through its violent and constant use in climbing, receives a permanent increase in strength. It becomes constructive instead of haphazard, so that instead of thinking what he might do a climber thinks more of what he could and may do. Each achievement makes the next one easier.

And so, sitting in our armchair by the fireside, we smile as our thoughts carry us back to Cambridge. It has been great fun. These last few weeks have been equal to the best of the old days in college, when to go out involved so little effort that we did so all too rarely. The trouble with the camera, the climbing, the excitement after each flash, the long car journey of over fifty miles up to Cambridge in the evening, night after night, and the return in the darkness before dawn, the hedgerows rushing past on the edge of vision, the feeling of control as the tyres gripped on each corner taken too fast, the moon shining her torch on a sleeping world, or the sense of the country around on a dark night; the memory of bad climbers forcing themselves to be brave on easy buildings, and good climbers arousing our admiration on the severe climbs; the feeling of knowing intimately all those with whom we have been out. Yes, it has been great fun.

Occasionally, as we pause in our reading to throw a log on the fire, we feel a vague unrest. It all seems too comfortable. The night is dark, and in its inscrutability tries to lead us on to action; or the moon laughs down, as though trying to tell us what she can see in other parts of the world. We stir in our chair, and wonder whether it is a sign of strength or weakness that makes us ignore the call. Cambridge is there, just over an hour from us, her roof-tops waiting.

While we pause, the wind rattles the casement more fiercely than ever, and seems to mock our hesitation. "You who sit there, action is life, and by your fireside you are ceasing to live. Shake the moth-balls from the old polo sweater you have always worn, and come out again. The night and I have always been your friends, do not desert us now. We will tell you secrets, as we used to tell you secrets in the past, and old friends will unite again." Thus he tempts us, and when we refuse he changes his tone, and accuses us of cowardice and lack of initiative. He raises uneasy phantoms, which claim to be our former selves and point accusing fingers at us as usurpers depriving a better self of its home.

Bringing all his guile into play, he begins to produce the desired effect. Doubts begin to assail us, tremendous fears of we know not what, and looking at the fender, our eyes grow large and round. Then someone enters the room, and we are our old laughing selves again. No one ever knows our deepest thoughts.

223

The Photographers' Farewell.

So we step out of one era into the next, and as we close the book it must remain closed for thirty years, until the time when the past begins to look longer than the future. There are others to follow; at this very moment there may be a dozen climbers on the buildings of Cambridge. They do not know each other; they are unlikely to meet. In twos and threes they are out in search of adventure, and in search of themselves. And inadvertently they will find what we found, a love for the buildings and the climbs upon them, a love for the night and the thrill of darkness. A love for the piece of paper in the street, eddying upwards over the roof of a building, bearing with it the tale of wood-cutters in a Canadian lumber-camp, sunshine and rivers; a love which becomes all-embracing, greater than words can express or reason understand.

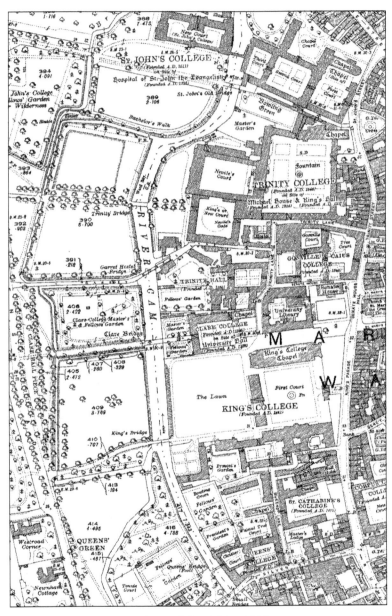

Map of Cambridge, 1927.

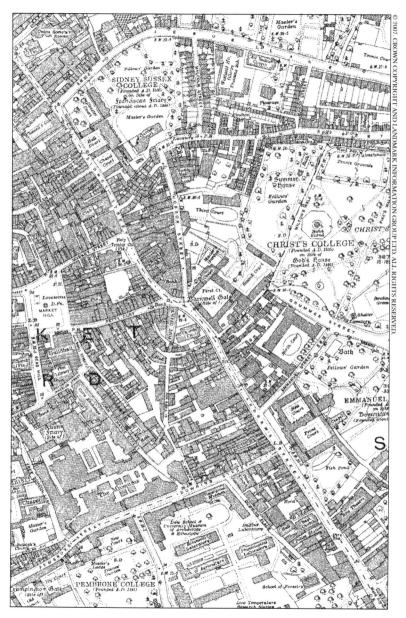

Map of Cambridge, 1927.

This book is typeset in 10.5pt Baskerville. The typeface was designed by John Baskerville in 1757, one year before he moved to Cambridge to become the University Printer, and was the typeface used in his masterpiece, the Folio Bible of 1763.

Printed in Great Britain
by Amazon